Spirit of the Wolf

Spirit of the Wolf

DISCOVERING THE TRANSFORMATIVE POWER OF LUPINE ENERGY

Art by Antonia Neshev

Words by Linda Star Wolf

with

Casey Piscitelli

STERLING ETHOS

New York

STERLING ETHOS
New York

An Imprint of Sterling Publishing
387 Park Avenue South
New York, NY 10016

© 2012 by Linda S. Wolf and Casey Piscitelli
Illustrations © 2012 by Antonia Neshev

ISBN 978-1-4027-8763-8

Distributed in Canada by Sterling Publishing
c/o Canadian Manda Group, 165 Dufferin Street
Toronto, Ontario, Canada M6K 3H6
Distributed in the United Kingdom by GMC Distribution Services
Castle Place, 166 High Street, Lewes, East Sussex, England BN7 1XU
Distributed in Australia by Capricorn Link (Australia) Pty. Ltd.
P.O. Box 704, Windsor, NSW 2756, Australia

Book design, layout, and editorial services: gonzalez defino, ny / gonzalezdefino.com

Photo credits: 18: Shutterstock / Lagui; 19: Library of Congress / LC-DIG-jpd-01487; 20:
Johannes Gehrts / Wikimedia Commons / Public Domain; 24: Library of Congress /
LC-USZ62-120094; 97: Shutterstock / Photosani

For information about custom editions, special sales, and premium and corporate purchases,
please contact Sterling Special Sales at 800-805-5489 or specialsales@sterlingpublishing.com.

Manufactured in China

2 4 6 8 10 9 7 5 3 1

www.sterlingpublishing.com

FOR AIDAN RAYNE
AND
CIAN SKY—
AND FUTURE WOLF PUPS EVERYWHERE

Contents

Introduction

Although the wolf has sometimes played a dubious role in our culture, in other cultures and in fairy tales he is a guide who can show us the way to rekindle ancient wisdom in our present-day lives. In our culture, the wolf has often been seen in the guise of the Big Bad Wolf or as the wolf that tried to eat Little Red Riding Hood and the Three Little Pigs. We've heard sayings such as "a wolf in sheep's clothing," which usually indicates that something apparently benign is, in fact, a sinister predator and perhaps evil in nature.

However, in indigenous or Native cultures, the wolf traditionally has been associated with many positive qualities—he may be the pathfinder, way shower, and community builder, exhibiting qualities such as loyalty, protection, and companionship. The wolf has also been seen in the role of visionary, teacher, and healer. It is said that he can guide us to deep inner self-discovery. These aspects may seem quite contrary to some of the stereotypical characteristics assigned to the wolf in popular culture.

However, the power of the wolf remains, and the general public has recently become more open to the positive aspects and nature of the wolf. Today it seems that one can't go into a gift shop or even a department store without seeing the emblem of the wolf on various items such as T-shirts, backpacks, posters, and book covers. Everywhere we turn, we find these images of the wolf. And the conversation about wildlife preservation becomes more animated every day, as people realize that it is necessary to defend the lives of wolves, especially in densely populated areas where the paths of wolves and humans frequently cross.

We might ask ourselves, "Why, all of a sudden, is there an infatuation with the wolf in popular culture?" However, before we explore that question in more depth, we should discuss the role of the wolf as it has evolved throughout history, beginning with its place in indigenous cultures.

Many Native American tribes and other indigenous cultures have had clans, and the Wolf Clan has been one of the most powerful. There have always been individuals (in both indigenous and nonindigenous cultures) that have felt called to or connected with particular clans. While most clans identify with an animal spirit, some embrace other natural or elemental spirits. For example, the Cherokee tribe included the Wild Potato Clan, known for farming and gathering, and the Blue Holly Clan, people who had a close connection to the healing power of herbs. Members of these clans often looked to these helping connections through visions, dreams, or perhaps even on a vision quest (vision quests will be discussed later).

In my own work, we utilize a process I have developed, known as the Shamanic Breathwork Journey, and many individuals report encountering animals during their breathwork experience. Even if a person has never heard of a spirit animal, totem, or ally, they will often begin to feel a kindred connection to a particular animal and find that it starts showing up in their outer life in a variety of ways. In sharing their breathwork journey with a facilitator or in a group, the journeyer may integrate their powerful experience and see how that animal might have a message for them. The animal may be guiding them to some sort of change—an answer or next step. Or it may be that the journeyers find themselves beginning to form relationships of trust, which will allow an animal to guide them.

Many relate visits from animal totems, whether in dreams or in transformative work, to the Jungian concept of archetypes. Carl Jung describes archetypes as part of the "collective unconscious"—common experiences and roles that all humans across all cultures and religions share. Your spirit animal guide may show up as a part of your own archetypal journey—to help you reconcile your inner child, mother, wise one, trickster, or other universal role that your spirit may take. Whether you look at this as a dreamtime experience or take such an experience more literally as a visitation from a powerful spirit animal connected directly to your soul's journey, it doesn't really matter. The important thing is how this encounter affects you and what guidance you might receive from this connection. In my own work, I encourage people to stay open and to not get hung up on whether something is metaphorical or literal. It's just as powerful one way or the other.

When people ask me whether I believe in spirit animals as an archetypal metaphor or as a real, tangible spirit totem, my answer is "Yes!" My own spiritual practice and path has led me to embrace the spiritual maxims from esoteric teachings that say, "As above, so below. As within, so without." Another way of saying this is, "On earth as it is in heaven (or the heavens)." The indigenous people of the world believed in a multitude of worlds or dimensions: the above, the middle, and the below—the visible and the invisible. They believed that everything with an existence in this world has origins behind the smoking mirror. Science tells us today that all matter has antimatter. Some branches of psychology explain that behavior comes from thoughts and feelings—invisible processes that result in outer actions, creating visible material results in the outer world. When we look at the world in that way, it is not much of a stretch to believe and understand that shamanic, metaphysical philosophies are not merely superstitions or even New-Age rhetoric.

Befriending one's animal totems, spiritual guides, and allies can truly serve as a higher function in personal transformation. In some indigenous cultures, elders would ask questions and watch small children interact with the natural world and the animals around them. They might notice that a child was drawn to a particular animal in nature—perhaps hunted a particular animal, drew that animal, or had dreams about it. Some tribes believed that you were born with animal protectors and guides, and that over time you would be drawn to other animals as well. New guides may reveal themselves to you as a part of your medicine through vision quests, dreams, meditation, or synchronistic, repeated encounters. Just as our relationships with fellow humans evolve over time, so do our relationships with our animal allies, depending on which medicines hold meaning for us in the present. We often find that, while some animal totems hold special meaning for us throughout our lives, others may fade or move into the forefront as we mature.

In some cultures, the belief system might not be that you were born with animal protectors, but that your spirit totems would choose you or show up in your life in some way. For instance, a bear might attack a young hunter. Rather than demonize the bear (provided the youth survived), others might think of him as having acquired bear medicine or bear energy from the encounter.

In certain traditions, if the animal shows up three or more times within a short period (usually no more than three days), it is said that the animal is offering you its medicine—a gift you may choose to receive or reject. An example of this could be that you flip on your computer and in your in-box someone unknown to you has sent a whole portfolio of pictures of owls. That same day, you go to the mailbox and, for no particular reason, find that a friend has sent you a card with a picture of an owl. Later that evening, as you are sitting on your patio you hear an unusual sound you aren't used to hearing and realize that it is an owl. If you are not paying attention, this gift might pass you by, and you might not even notice the synchronicity. On the other hand, if you have this knowledge in your conscious awareness, you would notice that the owl had appeared to you three times within a short period.

You may do one of several things: Do some research on the owl to see what its characteristics are; explore your own feelings about what the owl means to you, perhaps by journaling; or when you go to sleep that evening, suggest to your subconscious that Owl might come to you in a dream and give you a message. You could also simply meditate and breathe, as we did at the beginning of this chapter, allowing the image of Owl to come to you and give you a message or take you on an inner journey.

When a spirit animal offers you a gift, it is customary to offer gratitude. Perhaps while you are meditating or taking a walk, visualize Owl and say, "Thank you, brother/sister owl, for your good medicine, and I receive it gratefully." In some traditions, offering a pinch of tobacco or a pinch of cornmeal or burning sage or other herb is a way to offer the animal spirit ally your gratitude. Over the course of the next few days, weeks, and months, you could explore how to use the gifts of Owl or any animal that has appeared to you. Think of the bumper stickers that ask, "What Would Jesus Do?" or "What Would Buddha Do?" In this case, you might say, "What Would Wolf or Owl Do?" Allow your consciousness to evolve and answer that question for you.

I frequently receive e-mails and telephone calls from people asking questions about various animals—especially the wolf. People ask what it means if these animals are appearing in their lives. Before I answer that question, I sometimes ask the person what's actually happening in their life. Is there something unusual going on at this time? Are they undergoing some sort of major transformation, or have they been praying or asking or wishing for help? Have they been focused on some sort of burning issue or question? In Jungian psychology, it might be that the subconscious is sending you the answer through archetypal symbology and myth.

In the shamanic world, we would say that your soul has sent out a call and that your spirit animal has heard that call and is answering—the creator or source of the universe did not send us here to Earth to be alone. It sent us here along with many helpers and guides. Those who think that it might be strange to have a higher power in the universe send you a helper or ally in the form of an animal should reflect on the various traditions that believe a greater power has created guardian angels to watch over us. It is the same principle. The important point is the underlying assumption that there is a guiding force in the universe—our origin—that loves human beings enough to support our lives with visible and invisible helpers.

I remember speaking to a Mayan shaman, teacher, and friend once who frequently said "we" rather than "I" when preparing to do something. For instance, he would say, "We are going up on the mountain." After hearing him say this several times and seeing him head up the mountain by himself, I asked him, "Who is going with you?" He explained to me that, in his world, he never traveled alone. He told me he had many guides and allies, especially animal spirit totems that always traveled with him wherever he was. Continuing our journey, he asked me to visualize him with different animal totems walking on either side of him and flying above, behind, in front of, and actually within him. We visualized the animal spirit allies clearing obstacles, scouting, protecting, and alerting him to difficult or dangerous situations, heightening his senses and overall guidance.

This explanation helped me develop a much deeper connection with my animal totems and gain more respect for the ones with which I was beginning to work at that time. The Mayan shaman also told me how sorry he felt for people who had no connection to their animal totems and how alone they must feel. Chief Seattle once said, "What is man without the beasts? If all the beasts were gone, man would die from a great loneliness of spirit. For whatever happens to the beasts, soon happens to man. All things are connected." He had great compassion for the white man, who believed, as he put it, that he was alone without the support of the animal world. He noted what a lonely place the planet would be if all the animals were gone—not to mention that it would be the end of humanity because of our deep environmental and ecological connection and interdependence.

Perhaps because we spend so much time in homes, offices, and vehicles with windows shut and central heat and air-conditioning, our modern world has become very removed from the natural world. We are often blind to animals right outside our own doors. We've stopped feeling our connectedness to the animal kingdom and can no longer hear their voices in our psyches. In my mountain home in western North Carolina, I frequently hear the call of the red-tailed hawk screaming out as she flies over the river a short distance away, and I never fail to stop what I am doing to look heavenward, seeing her red feathers glinting in the sun, and to ask what message she is bringing me in that moment. The incredible synchronicity of whatever conversation I am having with someone or of the thoughts I am having at the moment the hawk calls never ceases to amaze me.

If human beings will develop a sense of humility—the word "humility" is derived from the Latin word *humus*, which means "earth" or "soil"—and realize that the animal kingdom actually consists of our elder brothers and sisters upon the planet, there is much wisdom we can gain by studying their behavior, learning their characteristics, and noticing their appearances in our lives.

In some ancient wisdom tradition teachings, human beings are thought of as the "new kids on the block." What that means is that the animal kingdom, the plant kingdom, and the mineral kingdom are all much older than humans by millions of years. They are, therefore, our elder brothers and sisters. They have been on Earth, engaged in an evolutionary process for millions of years, creating an environment that eventually allowed human beings to evolve in a sustainable world.

Most people understand from a scientific point of view that trees are instrumental in creating the right atmospheric conditions for us to breathe—a circular exchange in which they "inhale" our carbon dioxide exhalations and "exhale" oxygen for us to breathe. Recently, the scientific concern about the mysteri-

ous disappearance of bees became a worldwide concern. For without bees, many plants that rely on their pollination would perish. If there aren't any plants, there is nothing for animals to eat. Without plants or animals, there is nothing for humans to eat. In this way, our world consists of a web of extremely interdependent creatures. The plants are also dependent on the earth itself, as well as the mineral kingdom, to nurture their roots and create healthy individual plants that can feed and reproduce. All these things are connected.

In addition to spirit animals, many cultures have also developed ties to plant allies and to minerals and gemstones, such as crystals or the obsidian stone. Before you automatically think that a stone can't be your helper, remember all of the functions that crystals have in our lives today. They are used for amplification of sound frequencies in much of modern technology, as well as in computers. Long before crystals were used in this manner, wisdom-keepers in ancient civilizations used them to communicate with one another and as healing tools to change frequencies in people's bodies and aura fields. A piece of obsidian was often made into a blade or a pendant as protection or to cut away cords. The word "cord," used in this context, means an energetic tether. Shamanic people understood that these cords can actually be connected to negative qualities, such as negative thoughts or projections of others onto you or even your own negative thoughts from trauma. Cords may connect you to negative situations in your life from the past or present. In many indigenous cultures, it was not unusual to ask a healer for help in cutting these cords or attachments. That's when an obsidian blade or stone was used.

Although I won't go into further detail about plant and mineral allies in this book, it is important to understand that human beings are naturally connected to all aspects of the natural world. In fact, it's unnatural not to be! There is much wisdom and support to be gained by embracing our shamanic brothers and sisters of the natural world. They have already answered and perhaps perfected some of the questions we ask ourselves about our relationships and events in the modern world.

Now, back to the Wolf. We ask the question again: Why is it that the Wolf image, symbol, or archetype is appearing with such frequency in people's dreams and visions, and in films and elsewhere in popular culture? Perhaps the Wolf is coming into our collective consciousness at this time as a powerful archetype and spirit animal because of an unconscious prayer or call that we have sent out—a sort of distress signal. We live in a time of unprecedented environmental and climate change. Every day we see increasing signs of widespread social and political upheaval. Even the naysayers who have been skeptical about environmental change are beginning to sit up and pay attention to the accelerating fluctuation in weather patterns and the increase in natural disasters. In April 2011, there were a record 875 tornados in the United States, according to the National Oceanic and Atmospheric Administration. This surpassed the previous record for April of 267 tornados in 1974 as well as the record for tornados in any month (542 in May 2003). It is true that natural disasters have been a part of human existence for as long as we have been here, but the frequency and intensity of these occurrences cannot be ignored— tornados, record high and low temperatures, anomalies in rain-forest precipitation and river levels, disappearing ice caps, floods. During a weather forecast on the Weather Channel on June 2, 2011, meteorologist Carl Parker was struck by what he saw: very large and strong high-pressure ridges that were extremely unusual for that time of the year. He observed that this ridge dominated more than two-thirds of the country and reached very far north. The weather map that day, in Parker's words, "frankly, [had] climate change written all over it."

These are also trying times socially, as we have allowed greed to devour a political process that is meant to foster prosperity. The year 2010 saw the greatest economic disparities among U.S. citizens on record, and the U.S. dollar is in grave danger of being replaced as the world's reserve currency. Our political leaders seem more interested in advancing cultural agendas than addressing real-world problems. We saw tensions in the Middle East boil over in what has been dubbed the Arab Spring of 2011. Citizens of seventeen Arab countries took to the streets to protest corruption, oppression, and inequality. How these revolts will turn out remains an open-ended question, but what is clear is that we, as one people, will require inner guidance both to make the changes required for ourselves and to demand the changes from our leaders that are needed to emerge from this time of change. Are Wolf and other guides responding to our conscious and unconscious appeals for guidance in moving to a next phase of human existence—a time when we can advance humanity without violence against nature or ourselves?

A popular image of the wolf is either the lone wolf or a pack of wolves. The vision of the wolf on a full moonlit night, head arched backward and howling, invokes within us a feeling of desperate questioning or an appeal for aid—the feeling of the wolf calling out forlornly to the moon for answers, for help for the planet and all beings. It's as if the wolf has a connection to the great star nations.

Many indigenous people throughout history have held the belief that humankind has its origins in the stars. To name a few, the Cherokee are connected to the Pleiades, the Mayans were connected to the planet Venus, and the ancient Egyptians had a strong connection to the "Dog Star" Sirius. The wolf is the messenger between humanity and the ancient ancestor star beings. It's as if the wolf can, through its howling call, invoke not only the star nations but also the spirit world to bring assistance to Earth and her creatures. The wolf can also be seen as an aspect of our soul that calls out for help during the "dark night of the soul." In its calling, it is answered and given direction about which path to choose. Hence, the popular names for the wolf in the spirit tradition are Pathfinder and Visionary. I cannot think of a better spirit animal totem to emerge at this time. Wolf can offer a ray of hope for humanity and the planet as we continue our evolutionary journey through time and emerge into a new level of consciousness and expanded awareness.

As we observe the wolf, we learn how each member of the pack is valued and has a role within its circle. Seldom do we see what is referred to as the "lone wolf" unless it is scouting for the pack to find food or has set out to find a new pack. The wolf has learned that it is susceptible to danger and even just plain loneliness if it lives in isolation. Scientists say that if you see a lone wolf that is not scouting or perhaps protecting its pack, it is most likely in search of a new pack. As we will discuss later, this happens when there are unhealthy pack dynamics and when the need for the wolf to set out and transition to a new situation is the best thing for all.

In this way, the wolf's intuitive knowledge can help us find solutions to our own problems. We just need to find our way back to his guidance. ♣

1

Of Wolf and Humanity

Calling on the Spirit of the Wolf Totem

AND REKINDLING ANCIENT WISDOM

It is once again time to invoke the Wolf and call on its powers as a spirit totem animal. When invoking an animal totem or any other kind of totem, spiritual ally, or guide, I find it is best to sit or stand quietly, close your eyes, take a deep breath, and go into your internal world. Begin to let your external world and any distractions melt away as you practice breathing and dropping into your heart for a moment. This means simply coming out of your thinking mind for a moment and opening up to a more expanded state of consciousness so that you can become receptive and open and begin to listen to an inner voice. Perhaps, if you are so inclined, you may have inner visions and messages. So, at this time, as we begin this journey to connect with the Spirit of the Wolf together, I am doing just that—closing my eyes, going within, breathing, dropping into my heart, and calling the Spirit of the Wolf. I ask the Wolf, who is one of my power animal totems and my guide, to come and share its medicine with me and to convey its healing message for the world at this time. I ask that I may be a pure vessel, a "hollow bone" and channel of this great spirit animal, to be able to impart its message and wisdom for the world at this time.

*F*rom antiquity, wolves have been a central part of human existence. Ranging in the Northern Hemisphere from Eurasia to North America, wolves have by all accounts been interacting with humans for tens of thousands of years. Evidence of the powerful impact of the wolf on the human psyche is everywhere. Wolves show up in the ancient lore of the Native Americans, the Japanese, the Norse, and the Celts, to name a few. They are at once embraced as companions, respected as teachers, revered as gods, and feared as monsters.

Imagine yourself living thousands of years ago, perhaps somewhere in central Asia. Your existence is very different not only from your life today but even from that of Native Americans before European colonization. You are a hunter-gatherer. Humans have not yet learned agriculture and spend their days on the move, following the migration of prey animals, the availability of edible wild fruits and vegetables, and the cycles of the seasons. All you have are your weapons, your tools, your intellect, and your spirituality. You are inexorably entwined with Mother Nature. You experience the world in a purely visceral way. Like the animals with which you share the world, survival is always in the forefront of your mind—your next move, your next decision.

Yet you possess something uniquely human: your abstract mind. You are aware of the interconnection between everything in your environment: The humans, the animals, the plants, the earth and stones, the weather—and your mind doesn't draw a huge distinction between yourself and these other elements of nature. Unlike modern humans who experience a disconnect from the natural world and deny their dependence on it, you are immersed in nature and are under no such illusions. You look to nature for answers. You see animals with amazing abilities and senses that seem supernatural, and through a spiritual communion with them, you call upon the spirits of the animals to help and guide you. This spiritual alliance between early humans and animals is the birth of animal totems or animal spirit guides.

Indeed, animal totems seem to be as old as shamanism itself. The spirits of animal guides were a part of everyday life and spirituality as humanity evolved, called upon for help in summoning courage or empowerment, to affect the weather patterns, to heal the sick or wounded, to gain insight into the future, for vision and clarity, or to guide the dead into the afterlife. They were used to vanquish fear, to honor ancestors, and even to act as keepers of the heavens and the sun and the moon. Ancient lore tells us of a time when animals walked as men and spoke to us in our language. Could this be an abstraction of the vital role animal spirits played out in the hearts and minds of mankind? Was there a common dialogue in nature that all living creatures shared—a spiritual communion that allowed us to learn from each other and converse shamanically? Perhaps the stories in oral traditions of animals speaking to us are a carryover from the time when our senses were so attuned to nature that we possessed a direct line to the wisdom contained within the natural world.

There is every reason to believe that the wolf was at the center of our spiritual bond with the natural world. Nearly every culture within the natural range of the wolf possesses ancient myths and lore surrounding the wolf. One of the best-known examples of wolf lore is the legend of Romulus and Remus. In the Roman foundation myth, these twin humans were the offspring of the vestal virgin Rhea Silvia and the god Mars. Unwanted at birth, they were set adrift in the Tiber River. They eventually washed up on shore at the base of a fig tree, where, helped by a woodpecker (the wolf and the woodpecker were two animals favored by Mars), a she-wolf found them and suckled them along with her own cubs. Romulus and Remus would go on to become the founders of Rome, and the image of the twins suckling the mother wolf is one of the best-known symbols of the Roman empire.

Lupa Romana

Japanese lore yields many wolf myths and folk tales. The wolf was believed to be a messenger of the gods, specifically Yama-no-Kami, the god/goddess of mountains and fields. If one encountered a wolf and treated it kindly, the kindness would be returned, and the person would be blessed with the wolf's protection. It was believed that Yama-no-Kami offered the wolf as a protector of rice harvests and of the mountain forests. The wolf guarded the forests from unnecessary cutting of trees and from fires. [1] One Japanese folktale tells of a wolf that sits out-

Japanese woodcut depicting a wolf

side a house one night, listening to a man and his wife talking. The man says, "A leaky roof is to be feared more than a wolf." At the same time, a thief approaches the house and ascends the roof. The wolf runs away in terror, thinking that the thief is the "leaky roof" of which the man spoke. This story speaks to the way wolves were misunderstood.

Another story highlights the respect the Japanese had for the wolf, which is now extinct in that country. It tells of a suicidal man who goes into the mountains to be devoured by a wolf. He finds a wolf, but the wolf does not attack him. When he asks the wolf why, the wolf replies, "I only eat those who are animals disguised as humans." When asked how the wolf can tell the difference between a human and a shape-shifter, the wolf gives the man a hair off his eyebrow and tells him this will help him distinguish between the two. The man descends the mountain and, as night falls, finds an old house. He asks the people there for shelter. The old man agrees, but his wife refuses. The man takes out the eyebrow hair from the wolf, holds it up, and looks past it at the couple. He sees the old man,

[1] U. A. Casal, "The Goblin Fox and Badger and Other Witch Animals of Japan," in *Folklore Studies*, vol. XVIII (1959), pp. 1–93.

but standing next to him is an old cow instead of the wife. This story reveals how the wolf was thought to be a good judge of character and reinforces Japanese culture's respect for the wolf.

Germanic and Celtic lore are not without tales of the wolf, who appears as a being of both light and shadow. The Scottish Wulver was believed to be part man and part wolf. Not to be confused with a werewolf, the Wulver was thought to have lived on the Shetland Islands and was a kind, gentle creature. Legend says that it would catch fish and deliver them to the windowsills of the poor and hungry. Encountering the Wulver was a sign of good luck, and he would even help lost travelers by guiding them to the nearest town.

Some of the most intriguing wolf lore is that of the Germanic peoples, who came up with elaborate roles for the wolf within their pantheon. The primary Norse god Odin kept two wolves, Geri and Freki, as companions who cured him of his loneliness. The Norse also told of the wolves Skoll, who pursued the sun through the sky in the day, and Hati, who chased the moon across the night sky, giving us the daily cycle of light and darkness. In the legend of the Berserkers, ferocious warriors loyal to Odin called the Úlfhéðnar (wolf-coats) would work themselves into a frenzy and go to battle without protective armor. They were believed to have evoked the spirit of the warrior wolf (perhaps with the help of a narcotic and hallucinogenic salve) during a ceremony before battle. The legend tells of how

they were able to either turn into wolves or take on the magical qualities of wolves. Other Norse stories, perhaps the earliest known precursors to modern werewolf lore, tell of wolf shape-shifters. Although many of these Norse myths and legends delve into the darker aspect of Wolf Spirit, within them there seems to be an underlying theme of initiation. To these peoples, for better or worse, the wolf was a totem of strength and ferocity.

Odin with his two wolves, Geri and Freki

But why the wolf? Why has humanity projected its deepest admiration and its darkest fears upon this creature? To understand this we must again return to the earliest chapters in human existence. As hunters and gatherers, we inevitably would have been in close contact with wolves because, like us, they hunted in daylight and as a pack. In fact, no two species were more alike in this way. It is not hard to imagine early humans regularly encountering wolves while hunting and possibly even competing for some of the same prey animals. In the wake of our hunt, wolves learned that the carcasses of our prey were easy sources of food.

Wolf packs began to follow human hunting parties. There is little doubt that wherever there were humans, there were also wolves. In return for the leftover spoils of hunting, the wolves provided early humans with inspiration. They were the object of our spiritual longing. These were mysterious creatures, swift of foot and with keen senses, that could hunt cooperatively and successfully without the benefit of speech, gestures, or weapons. As we entered new and unfamiliar lands, we would have taken cues from wolves. Human hunters would have followed packs of wolves, as they had an uncanny ability to track prey animals and predict their migratory patterns. The relationship was mutually beneficial, and scientists and archaeologists alike agree that early human populations grew much faster because of our symbiosis with the wolf.

Then something happened that would change the course of humanity forever. We began to notice that some wolves, while shy, showed neither fear nor aggression when they entered our camps. Whereas the majority of wolves would keep their distance from humans, encroaching upon only the outermost fringes of our presence, these few wolves would enter the camps in search of food. They even showed a strange curiosity about humans. Humans must have been intrigued and humbled by these emboldened creatures.

The next twist in the story of wolves and man remains a mystery. Somehow we began to domesticate them. Perhaps it happened organically, as groups of these fearless wolves began congregating and breeding around human populations. Perhaps we were able to catch and keep only those wolves that were brave enough to get close to us and then to breed them. However it may have begun, over many

generations we bred wolves while selecting against aggression and fear. We allowed only the most docile wolves to breed, and with each new generation, the wolves became more domesticated.

The domestication of wolves marks a pivotal time in human history. We now had our loyal companions, the ancestors of modern domesticated dogs. Indeed, the study of mitochondrial DNA in domestic dogs shows that every species of domestic dog is a direct descendant of *Canis lupus*, the gray wolf. What is more fascinating is that this process began much earlier than most people imagine. The same mitochondrial DNA studies reveal that the process of domestication in wolves began more than 100,000 years ago. That means that, even well before we first domesticated wolves, we had been coexisting with them. With that in mind, we can begin to understand why wolves have such a deep-seated place in the human psyche.

To this day, wolf energy is called upon in many spiritual practices, including in modern-day shamanism. This is in large part due to the role wolf medicine has played in Native American traditions. As Europeans colonized the North American continent and the Native peoples were killed and marginalized by the thousands, their spiritual practices were shunned and even made illegal. Many Native peoples were converted to Christianity. However, the beliefs, teachings, rituals, and ceremonies of old were not completely lost. The latter part of the twentieth century saw the beginnings of an age of tolerance, and many people of non–Native American heritage began to explore and embrace the ancient teachings of the tribes. Among these teachings was animal medicine and the use of spirit totems— the belief that one could commune with the spiritual essence of the animal and call upon that energy for teaching, healing, guidance, courage, vision, or any specific qualities ascribed to that particular animal.

It is difficult for many people today to understand how animals could have been so revered. The key is to realize that, in contrast to modern views of animals as lesser beings, animals were viewed as members of the various "Four-Footed Tribes." Rather than being seen as "other" than us, animals were considered to be of equal value—they were our brothers and sisters. These Native American traditions were your authors' introduction to animal spirit totems, and the majority of the teachings explained in this book come from that context.

The wolf is arguably the most revered animal in Native American spiritual practices; it shows up in the myths and legends of nearly all tribes. The Zuni, a Pueblo tribe, honor Wolf as one of the six directional keepers. The Zuni keep small fetish stones in the shape of the wolf in which the spirit of the animal resides. These fetishes are used in prayer, for success in hunting, and to honor the wolf and its qualities of loyalty, particularly as it relates to the importance of family. In Shoshone tradition, Wolf is a wise deity. A Shoshone proverb, which harks back to the days when animals walked as men, tells how Coyote harbored resentment against Wolf because Wolf was revered and honored by the people. After hearing of how Wolf can resurrect the dead by shooting an arrow beneath them, the trickster Coyote warns Wolf that doing this would soon cause the world to

Cheyenne wolf dance

be overpopulated. Realizing that this is merely a trick by Coyote to cause Wolf to fall from favor with the people, Wolf agrees, knowing that Coyote's plan will one day backfire. So when Coyote's son is fatally bitten by a poisonous snake, Wolf reminds him of his words and refuses to resurrect his son. This was the first time death fell upon the land.

The Blackfoot legend of the Wolf Man tells of a man with two spiteful wives who moved far away from the tribe to a place where he might teach them right and wrong away from the influence of others. Resentful of their isolation, the wives decided to kill him. The wives trapped the man in a deep hole, left him to die, and returned to their people in mourning, with a story of how their husband had died while hunting. A wolf discovered the man near death and, after calling the other wolves as well as many other animals for council, decided to rescue the man and bring him into the pack. An old, blind wolf with powerful medicine restored the man's health and transformed his head and hands into those of a wolf, leaving the rest of his body unchanged. With his knowledge of man, the Wolf Man helped the pack steal meat from the snares of the people, but the people captured him one day and recognized him, despite his changed appearance. He told the people of his wives' conspiracy, and the wives were judged and never seen again.

In addition to including the wolf in their lore, Native Americans honored the animal by naming their clans after it. Indeed, while the function of each clan differs, the Wolf Clan is the most commonly shared clan among the various tribes. Native American tribes that have Wolf Clans include the Tsimshian, Wyandot, Iroquois, Cherokee, Creek, Shawnee, Chippewa, and many others. The wolf was revered enough to be the primary symbol of such tribes as the Munsee (Lenni Lenape), the Mohegan, and the Skidi (Pawnee), whose name is derived from the Pawnee word for "wolf."

The Seneca nation is the largest of the Iroquois member nations, and the Seneca Wolf Clan is one of its eight clans. One of the Seneca Wolf Clan's greatest teachers in the recent past was Twylah Hurd Nitsch, Seneca Wolf Clan Grandmother and elder. Grandmother Twylah demands attention in this book because she was among the first Native teachers to advocate the inclusion of non-Natives in Native American traditions and spirituality. She was, in fact, the spiritual grandmother to your authors. Without her, the path that led your authors to this work would not have been cleared. I (Linda Star Wolf) was connected to her for many years before she passed in 2007. She was responsible for collecting, organizing, and writing down many of the Seneca oral teachings. As a Wolf Clan elder, she spoke often to others and me about the importance of walking on a path of integrity, stability, dignity, truth, love, wisdom, and trust. She said that these were all qualities that the wolf embodied in its highest aspects. With a twinkle in her eye and a humorous voice, Gram would say, "If the wolf has called you, there is no escaping!" Her meaning is that if a wolf totem or guide begins to synchronistically appear to you in your daily life or in your dreams and meditations, this energy is appearing for an important reason. You begin to notice that the wolf is appearing to you with great frequency. Perhaps someone gives you a picture of a wolf or you turn on the television and it is broadcasting a documentary on wolves—it feels as if the wolf is, as she would put it, "dogging your tracks."

We have established that wolves have been with us since our earliest times and that cultures across the globe have been captivated and inspired by them enough to include them in their written and oral histories, their pantheons, and their societies. Looking into the past, it seems natural that humans would have been fixated on this creature, given our close interaction with nature and reliance on the land—but are there any additional lessons to be learned from Wolf for modern humans? As we head into the twenty-first century, what could our wild brother—pushed to the margins of his once-expansive territory by our sprawl—have to teach us about being human?

In the chapters to come, we will invoke Wolf to do just that. As indigenous peoples have been doing for thousands of years, we will call forth the various aspects and characteristics of Wolf and experience them through our own spirituality. Each chapter will begin with an invocation—a type of meditation calling forth that specific aspect of Wolf Spirit. You will also notice that the aspects build upon each other. We will explore how wolves live in community and show us humans how to be productive members of our communities and the value in doing so.

Next, we ask Wolf to show us how to be visionaries—to look beyond our waking consciousness for inspiration. Then Pathfinder Wolf helps us bring that vision into our bodies and also to honor the paths of others while maintaining our boundaries. Guide Wolf teaches us to follow our path, whatever it may be, with truth and to look inward and ask ourselves if we are living with integrity. Shadow Wolf calls on our courage—courage to face those dark aspects of ourselves that we have chosen not to claim as our own, courage perhaps, if our current situation isn't healthy, to set out on our own as a lone wolf in search of a new purpose. Finally, we learn the value of nurturing and being nurtured as individuals, community members, and stewards of the planet. As you read on with an open mind, identify with these aspects in terms of where you are on your own journey. Wolf energy always has something to offer for the seeker who intentionally opens her heart to higher understanding.

With the help of a contributor, Samuel Breidenbach, we will also look at some distinct wolf behaviors that may go a long way in explaining our bond with the animals. As a biologist and wolf zoologist, Breidenbach has spent years observing wolf behavior, and as a mystic, he draws deeper learning from his encounters with wolves.

With our clear intention, we will access the common plane we share with the wolf. Wolf Spirit has been guiding our ancestors for millennia—the lessons reside deep within our DNA—and we intend to begin to unlock them. We owe a great debt of gratitude for all that the wolf has taught us—knowledge we now are in danger of taking for granted. Perhaps it is now time for us to repay that debt by once again honoring the wolf instead of persecuting our shamanic brother ever closer to extinction. Our aim is to share the heart and soul of the Wolf Spirit and our interconnectedness, which may have been forgotten but has not been lost since the passing of a time when we shared a close physical communion with the wolf. Wolf is a powerful totem, and it once again comes to lead us forward on our path of spiritual and human evolution. 🐾

2

Community

Community

Great Spirit of the Wolf who watches over, protects, and creates social order within your pack, we call upon your wise wolf ways so that we may know how to relate to one another in a sacred manner that will promote peace and harmony within our own human pack as well as with all beings and nature. May we respect one another and honor the impact we have upon each other's lives through our actions. May we always remember that every one of us is a valuable member within our human family with something important to contribute to the community. May the wisdom of your community Wolf Spirit teach us how to live in balance with one another and to enjoy the many aspects of community life—the support, the companionship, the protection, and the playfulness. All of these gifts of community, or pack, living help us to create a deeper connection to those we value and love and to understand those that are different from us.

As we open to your innate understanding of how to continue the sacred circle of life, may we each be filled with the inner knowing and sense of belonging that is so important to all beings and to recognize the many gifts we that receive from one another and will pass on to future generations.

*C*entral to human emotional and spiritual well-being are our roles in our communities. Early humans found great success in forming communities. Our ancestors began to flourish when we moved from a nomadic way of living to having cohesive, permanent social groups. Agriculture, irrigation, sophistication of tools and weapons, and rapid population growth are all associated with our realization of the value of community. However, more than that, a sense of being part of a community seems to fill a basic human need—to fit in and to be a cog in the wheel of something greater than ourselves. This is our natural state, and we experience dysfunction when we are isolated or otherwise estranged from our roles in our communities. How has our sense of community changed over time, though? What is your role in community?

Our ancestors understood better than we do that we are all connected and share a common fate as a species. What benefited the community benefited us and would ultimately benefit our descendants. Most of us who live in the modern, developed world have compartmentalized our roles into various communities. Indeed, apart from our neighborhoods, towns, and cities, most of us are a part of many communities. If you work long hours away from home, your professional community may be a central part of your life, even though it is far away geographically. Your network of friends is another community. Perhaps you have a vast social-networking community. How many of your friends on social-networking sites do you talk to regularly or have a meaningful relationship with? Ironically, as the number of communities we form grows, we begin to think small in terms of their importance. As they are segmented, our roles as members of a community can become the means to serve only our interests, and the larger picture is blurred. If you were asked to think of your most important community, what would come to mind?

There is a shift in consciousness that has been picking up steam over the past several decades. It is a realization of a lost wisdom based on the interconnectedness of all beings that inhabit this planet. The Wolf Spirit aspect of community can help us remember this lost wisdom. The behaviors of individual wolves within a pack invariably serve the greater good. Even behaviors that may appear selfish or

aggressive, such as an assertion of dominance, can have outcomes that are ultimately beneficial. For example, would it serve the pack if the strongest wolf did not assert its dominance? Similarly, do you have untapped strengths that would serve your community? Wolf can show us how to step into our power, and that doing so is not only OK but also part of being a responsible community member.

Samuel Breidenbach offers some insight into Wolf's community structure:

> *The community the wolf lives in is really no different in complexity than humans living in a modern urban setting. It has some different rules and is perhaps less forgiving, as there are few social safety nets in place—that is, except for the wolves' family, and here is where Canis lupus excels.*
>
> *Different species of animals use different evolutionary strategies to prosper. Tigers are solitary hunters for the most part, and that approach to existence has worked for them for several million years. Horses have a herd structure, with only one main male stallion and many mares and colts. And birds pair up to raise their young and then flock most of the rest of the year with unrelated others. But the wolf actually employs many strategies, and most have to do with the biological family they are born into—that is, except for the males, who act like pollen in plants and migrate away from the family as far as they can go so that they can spread their genetic heritage far and wide. No matter where the male goes, though, the social unit of a wolf is still based on the family unit.*
>
> *The family unit model has been demonstrably so successful for wolves that nearly all North American indigenous peoples have copied them in their family, clan, and tribe strategies. And there is a reason for this. A solitary hunter is only as good as his worst day of hunting. If injured or a victim of a freak natural disaster, he has very little help to fall back on. But a family always has at least two members, and is often a greatly extended clan composed of older brothers, sisters, aunts, uncles, and so on. Biologists and zoologists today continue to find new and unexpected complexities in the family structure of wolves.*

Scientists have observed that sometimes when an alpha (leader) male is sick or injured, another male wolf will often step in temporarily to help out as the leader. If the alpha recovers, the other goes back into his place in the pecking order with no fuss. Apparently, this is for an altruistic motive as even if the leader dies, this individual does not often become the new leader. Only humans are also known to use this sophisticated leadership strategy.

As a wolf biologist studying the wolves in Denali National Park in Alaska, I have observed such complex behavior relating to the community of wolves with their individual families, subpacks and packs, and then on into super packs that I had a difficult time figuring out how it all worked. The wolves apparently had it all sorted out, however, as there was almost always a smooth transition from being an alpha male in a family to being a lower-ranking wolf in a larger system.

Again, it is only the most highly intelligent and adaptive human who does anything similar to this in complexity, and it is no wonder that this system has been copied by our ancestors for tens of thousands of years. We are in many ways two-legged wolves in our social structures.

Clearly, the wolf helped contribute to our heritage by teaching us a successful model of social cohabitation. Perhaps Wolf Spirit can help us learn a larger lesson about how to better evolve into a healthy, functional global community. Just as our ancestors adopted leadership and subordinate roles modeled after the wolf-pack hierarchy, we can now view these roles in the context of the world community. When we look at community structures, it is true that the whole of the community is greater than the sum of its parts. This is because of a synergistic effect when, just as a wolf pack does, we come together toward a common goal. A wolf pack may have the fastest runner, the most skilled hunter, or the fiercest fighter, but the strength and ultimate success of the pack depends much more on the cohesiveness of the pack as a whole than on any one member. It is also true that, taken out of that pack structure, even the strongest of wolves will not be able to survive long unless it finds another pack to join. 🐾

3

Visionary

— INVOCATION —

Visionary

*W*e call to the bright shining spirit of the Visionary Wolf and invite you, oh sacred one, into our dreams, meditations, and inner journeys so that we too may see within our mind's eye with the eyes and heart of the Wolf. Oh Visionary Wolf, if ever there was a time for humanity to "cry out for a vision" and to learn your messages that would lead humanity forward into a new era built with the true vision of what will sustain all of life on this Mother Earth, it is now. We open ourselves on all levels—body, mind, and spirit—so that we may receive the gift of your visionary powers. May all our senses, both outer and inner, be activated and attuned in a good way so that we may pick up the path of the heart, one that will lead us to truth, love, and wisdom for each of our paths and the world around us.

🐾 🐾 🐾

*T*he Visionary Wolf is the one who knows how to move beyond the ego mind and to see into other dimensions and realms. Think of individuals who fit this category: the Albert Einsteins, Henry Fords, Leonardo da Vincis, Charles Darwins, and others who report that they gained inspiration for their vision through mystical means. Often these epiphanies were sweeping and grand, but other visions were very detailed and did not have the sort of abstract nature we associate with vision. As if receiving a gift from the ether, some of the greatest minds in history simply "downloaded" incredibly creative ideas on how to give birth to things that had never before been fathomed. Edgar Casey said, "Dreams are today's answers to tomorrow's questions." Einstein dreamed, whether awake or asleep, in pictures. His famous theory of relativity was inspired when he began to imagine himself riding on a beam of light.

Some have speculated that these unique thinkers had what could be considered borderline mental-health issues, such as schizophrenia or autism. Often they had difficulties as children, as it seems the same condition that troubled them also gave rise to their groundbreaking ideas. Take, for example, St. Hildegard von Bingen. This revered visionary from the Middle Ages was held in high regard in the Catholic Church at a time when very few women were respected for their opinions. She shared her visionary revelations on matters of spirituality, the natural world, music, and even sex after what many agree were bouts of debilitating migraine headaches.

Being a visionary encompasses many areas. It boils down to imagining beyond this moment: To a moment in time that has not yet passed but that is as real as the past itself. To bring the vision into this realm. To evoke the vision into material form. To bring it to pass. It is a quality that indigenous peoples have attributed to the wolf. Imagine the sense of awe with which our ancestors, who had no knowledge of science or biology, must have looked upon the wolf. Indeed, even to modern science, much is still a mystery about the wolf's seemingly supernatural senses. The sensitive ears that hear well beyond the range of human ability (up to ten miles in the open), the sense of smell that can warn of danger and detect prey from up to two miles away, and the vision that allows wolves to see at night and to detect minute movements as they stealthily hunt. But still, while these keen, heightened senses are seen throughout nature and can be somewhat understood by science, it appears that the wolf also possesses extrasensory abilities.

Imagine yourself, again, in the time of the nomadic ancients as one of the first of our kind to coexist with the wolf. You and a small hunting party are out in search of prey, determined to find the next meal for your families, as you spot another hunting party in the distance—a hunting party of wolves. You track and stalk the wolves for miles, hoping to close ground and eventually confront the animals and kill them. As you follow their tracks to the top of a hill and through the woods into a clearing, you find the wolves engaged in hunting a herd of reindeer. You and your team watch as the wolves skillfully and cooperatively hunt the herd and soon realize that your original prey has led you to a much more bountiful treasure. Having hunted the area for years, you know that the herds have never in your lifetime taken this particular route, and after your hunt you reflect with wonder on just how the wolves knew where and when to intercept the herd. Breidenbach touches on this:

> *It has long been known to scientists and indigenous peoples that the wolf has some indefinable senses, understandings, or dream visions that defy conventional wisdom. A good example is in the Northwest Territories of Canada and in Alaska, where the wolves seem to know days in advance when the migrating caribou will be in a particular area. It is so well known in some areas that the local hunters can tell by the excitement or calls of the wolves that the large deer species will be there, in spite of the fact that the herd does not always go a particular way, direction, or into a specific given area. Yet the local wolves know where they will be and when.*
>
> *The local shamans, or wise men, have told me that the wolves see the herd in their "dreams" and so always know where they are. They tell me that this has always been so and that the wolves were the beings who taught the early humans who watched, observed, and listened to these pack hunters how to also dream of prey animals and food sources. In*

fact, they claim that if the wolves' wisdom has not been passed on to the people, the people would not have survived. Not only could the wolves dream where the food was; they apparently could also know much else, like the coming weather or if a particular wolf, prey animal, or even human was sick. This is the Visionary Wolf at its best as far as we humans are concerned.

It is important to realize, as we contemplate the importance of animal totems, that our ancestors didn't just learn explicitly from watching wolf behavior, although that was an important part of our heritage from the wolf. They invited in the wolf energy through esoteric spirituality. They believed that they took the extrasensory powers and sensitivities into their own being. This is what is meant by spiritual communion.

We need only look into our recent past to see examples of visionary figures who accomplished great things that were unlikely or seemingly impossible. Mahatma Gandhi, through his teachings of nonviolent resistance and focus on self-empowerment, provided the inspiration and the impetus to the people of India to resist British imperial control. His teachings and three pivotal nonviolent movements set the foundation for the end of the British Raj (British rule of India). How could this strictly peaceful movement be so effective in a violent atmosphere that didn't extend that same courtesy to him and his people?

How could Martin Luther King Jr. have given such momentum to a burgeoning civil rights movement in a very young country with a history steeped in slavery and segregation—a United States that took for granted institutionalized racism in the form of interracial marriage bans; segregated lunch counters, public transportation, schools, and workplaces; and banks unwilling to loan to minorities. His "dream" was his vision. He knew the demise of these injustices would come to pass, just as he knew he would not live to see them. Indeed, the day before his death, Dr. King spoke of how he would love to live a long life but that he was "not concerned about that now. I just want to do God's will. And He's allowed me to go up to the mountain. And I've looked over. And I've seen the Promised Land.

I may not get there with you. But I want you to know tonight, that we, as a people, will get to the promised land!" This well-known speech can give us insight into true vision—King's acknowledgment that he simultaneously knew his time would be short and the cause would prevail.

Wolf energy teaches that vision is going higher than your present circumstance, seeing things that others argue will never come to pass. Art Berg is an inspirational figure who battled his way back to health after a crippling car accident and moved on to inspire many through his writing. He popularized the motto "The difficult we do immediately, the impossible takes a little longer"—a perfect example of clear, faithful vision. William Blake said, "What is now proved, was once only imagin'd." And Carl Jung spoke of vision when he said, "Without this playing with fantasy, no creative work has ever yet come to birth. The debt we owe to the play of the imagination is incalculable."

Just as Wolf's innate vision serves the greater good of his pack, we must call on Wolf to help us access our vision to serve our global community. "A new type of thinking is essential if mankind is to survive and move toward higher levels." This quote from Albert Einstein shows his vision, for in the years since he lived our priorities as a human race have focused on segmented self-interest instead of long-term sustenance and commonality.

If we want to solidify a shift, if we want to raise consciousness, we must be visionaries. This is not an undertaking for a special few. It's time for each of us to embrace that quality. We must appreciate our past and use it to envision a new future. These great visionaries were people who, for whatever reason, were able to cultivate their vision to its fullest extent. We do not know whether they were born with an inherent predisposition for clear vision or their unique life circumstances helped develop it. However, we all possess the ability to manifest our vision if we nurture our truth, and calling upon animal totems is a valuable tool for achieving this.

The future is accessible right now—encoded in all living beings just as the oak is encoded in the acorn. The physical human form is a vastly complex system. Our entire architecture—all of the information we will ever need to grow and

form our bodies and minds—is present at the moment of conception, and each of our cells contains that vast blueprint. It is a system we may never be able to fully understand, so perhaps the best way to access some of the most mysterious truths about our being is through vision rather than science. Our human form is a dense collection of energy existing on a space-time continuum. Is it really a stretch to believe that we are capable of manifesting a better future for ourselves through vision and faith in that vision?

One way we can vision is by participating in disciplines such as meditation and creative visualization. We can participate in shamanic journeys that take us to unexplored parts of our psyches. Some people get their clearest visions in their dreams. Many artists, musicians, authors, philosophers, and the like receive their clearest insights in that twilight period just after waking from a dream. Just as in the earlier example of Albert Einstein, who stumbled upon the inspiration for his theory of relativity, we can surprise ourselves if we take time to open our unconscious minds to greater experience.

Invite Visionary Wolf into your being. Become the wolf and find something that perhaps you did not even know you were looking for in the first place. Finding your vision and ultimately your path is for the good of all, in addition to being good for you. Call in the keen senses of the wolf. Make your mind quiet, and open all layers of your consciousness so that your wolf guide may hint toward the distant hill over which a new vision awaits you. 🐾

Pathfinder

4

Sacred Path

Wolf Spirit as Pathfinder, we petition you from our heart's deepest longing to hear our wolf howls as we call out to you, asking that you show us the way to our sacred purpose on Earth at this time. May each of us be open to letting go of our ego attachments to who we thought we were and to becoming willing and teachable so that we may have the courage we need in order to speak our truth in the world. Lead us on this great journey of life, always with integrity and dignity as we learn by your example how to seek out, discover, and follow the path that is truly ours to take. Show us how to step out willingly onto the sacred path as we walk around the great medicine wheel of life and death and rebirth and face our fears so that we may embrace what is ours to do in the world. May all beings know that there is a sacred path and that we only need to listen to your voice in the wind and follow our wolf nose in order to find the scent that will lead us homeward.

*T*he importance of infusing ourselves with vision is to become inspired to manifest our soul purpose—so that we do not fall into old patterns or squander our energy and time by creating something that is simply ego-based. It is not enough to just dream. It requires a greater wisdom shared by all great visionaries to move things forward and not fall into old patterns of thinking. Wolf is a being of action, and we can call on Wolf Spirit to help us discover the path to manifesting our vision. Many New-Age disciplines are caught in the quagmire of *spiritual bypass*, a term coined by psychologist John Welwood that refers to the dysfunctional practice of relying on spiritual discipline in order to avoid dealing with practical problems. This occurs when one's vision—discovering and holding it—is the ultimate goal. You go inside and find your soul's purpose, and that's it for the rest of your life! However, the next natural step on our human path is to take that vision from our hearts and minds and bring it into our bodies. If you are familiar with the system of energetic centers in the human body, this relates to the lower chakras—survival, sexual, and grounding energy. This is where we create. This is where our dreams become material.

Pathfinder Wolf teaches us that we have a responsibility to not only follow our own path but to also honor all paths. Remember what Wolf teaches us about right relationships in the community: Each member contributes to the pack by walking with dignity on their own path while at the same time respecting the roles of others. This is true of all pack members on all levels of the pack hierarchy. While realizing these truths implies a measure of responsibility to community, it can also be freeing in that we can focus on bringing our vision into light and don't need to carry the weight of others on our shoulders. Just as a nerve cell in your little toe does not need to worry about creating a heart muscle, all we have to know is what our part is. And if we have done the appropriate journeying through our hearts, we know what is ours to do. This path may change over time—just as in the wolf pack, where roles within the pack change over time. The most important thing, however, is to remain open to greater wisdom, following with dignity a path that leads toward your soul purpose. Carlos Castaneda said, "Follow the path with heart." Follow it, but if it ceases to have meaning for you, change it! You may find that in order to right the ship, you may need to go back to being a visionary again. We spoke about spiritual bypass, and it applies here as well.

It is important to remember that whatever your path in life, it should always—will always, if you are following your soul purpose—possess the flavor of who you are. For example, perhaps when you were young, you decided to be a carpenter. Later in life, you went to school to be an architect. After years of working as an architect, you've decided to use your skills to build sustainable communities. The path has changed over time but it always has had a flavor of who you were at your core. It may not always be clear where the ultimate destination is, and it is not important.

Some may say that it is not always practical to follow vision. It's true that sometimes you just need to survive—maybe you need to get a job or go to school or move away or do something else that doesn't immediately serve the dream. Indeed, sometimes you may have to do that. However, be sure that while you are fulfilling these basic needs you are also, on the side, doing what you need to do to advance on your path. Otherwise, you may find yourself caught up and stuck. You may find you have fallen into depression or are lost in some sort of addiction, whether it's alcohol, drugs, relationships and sex, or food. Knowing and following your path gives you self-esteem and motivation.

Following one's path also requires strong boundaries. It is true that wolves are peaceful and nurturing creatures. However, respect for boundaries within the pack as well as between different packs is paramount in wolf behavior. In the context of the pathfinder aspect, a wolf's role within the pack can be viewed as its path. Pack hierarchy, then, is the strict system of enforcing boundaries so that each wolf is secure in its role. Four types of boundaries are evident here: boundaries for the self, not allowing self-destructive behaviors to alter your path; boundaries for others, not allowing others to violate you; respecting others' boundaries, not neglecting your own journey for the sake of another; and boundaries for the community.

Wolf Spirit teaches us that our paths are sacred and that part of walking our path with integrity is respecting it enough to stay on it. We all face temptations to stray, as any journey worth making will be hard. The strength of our journey

lies in our ability to avoid self-defeating behaviors. We must decide what actions are acceptable to us. We must draw a circle around our center representing our boundary. Within that circle are things we accept, and outside it are situations we choose to avoid. Just as our path may change over time, so may our boundary circle, and the things we place outside our boundaries can be thought of as "not now" or "not ever" items. Perhaps we struggle with some sort of addiction and choose to put that addiction outside the circle in "not ever" status. At the same time, we choose to put the triggers or people who have contributed to the addiction in the "not now" category until we are secure enough to let them back within our boundaries. When we evoke wolf energy, we are not ashamed or afraid of setting these boundaries for the sake of honoring our path. When we do this with confidence, the energy of that boundary emanates from us and can be felt by those around us.

We must first learn to set boundaries for ourselves and then set boundaries for others. Some people find it is much less difficult to exercise self-control than it is to not allow others to affect them. Wolves mark their territory, and in the same way, the way we carry ourselves can create an aura that gives the impression of our boundaries, so that others will be less likely to even try to cross them. However, if someone does infringe on our path, we can show them in clear terms that this will not work for us. Again, Wolf communicates its limits unapologetically.

The morality of respecting others' boundaries is self-evident. We may challenge someone's position or disagree with them, but forcing our will against another is inherently unhealthy. Wolves understand this. This is why while intra-pack challenges to establish dominance are common, severe injury or the killing of another wolf is extremely rare, and inter-pack wars and spontaneous violence against other animals are never observed in the wild.

Another commonly misunderstood aspect of respecting boundaries is the necessity of avoiding codependency. It is our responsibility to follow our path. This means not falling into the trap of caring more about others than about our own journey. This is codependent behavior, and it is self-destructive. It is important to remember that we can honor others, support them, and even sometimes sacrifice for them as long as we can stand in our own truth while doing so. Codependent behavior is a kind of boundary violation. When we respect others, we must honor their ability to make choices for and take care of their selves.

A good example of this kind of behavior can be found in the dynamics of addiction. The saying goes that for every addict, there are at least ten people enabling him. Often loved ones of addicts, in an attempt to help or save them, enable them with emotional, financial, or other types of support that in fact make the situation worse. The addict is able to continue using without "hitting bottom" and therefore has no incentive to stop the addictive behavior. Perhaps jail time, eviction, or a trip to a rehabilitation center would be the best possible thing to happen to the person, precipitating the kind of motivation necessary to get that person back to a healthy path. Healthy, loving support—without codependency and enabling behaviors—may seem harsh, but it is the only way to maintain respect for everyone's boundaries. Crossing the boundaries of others is acceptable only when our paths intersect.

Finally, we can also hold boundaries for our communities. Ultimately, our paths allow us not only to better ourselves, but to improve our communities as well. As we approach boundary issues with truth and integrity, we automatically advance the world around us. By aspiring to strong morals and character traits in our own lives, we identify that which is worth fighting for as a society. Just as wolves mark and patrol the boundaries of their territories, we can learn to be sentinels and perhaps even warriors so that our pack can survive and thrive. Sometimes it is necessary to stand up and make clear what is and what is not acceptable. When a disruptive or unbalancing force has encroached upon societal boundaries, wolf medicine is about being assertive and unafraid. ❧

5

Guide

Great White Wolf

Great White Wolf sitting calmly in the North of the sacred wheel of life, are you calling me to sit with you on this warm summer night? I cannot refuse your noble request and must find my way to be by your side no matter what the risk. For it is such a great honor to have one's name called by the greatest teacher of all. You are the one I have seen in my dreams, and at times I have heard your soft footfalls tracking me when I was lost. I have made the great journey around this spiraling wheel and learned life's lessons of what is false and what is real. I humbly surrender to your wise guidance and humbly ask you to show me the way as I let go of the past and step into my future on this very day. For to carry the Spirit of the Wolf is one of the greatest gifts ever to be received, and all of your sacred qualities now live inside me. With integrity and stability, I will stand on your holy ground as I lift my face heavenward and send out a mighty sound reminding me just who I really am. As I remember, so too will others, and that is the biggest gift of gratitude I can give back to you. This is the time for you to regain your rightful place in history and to lead us all back to dignity. Oh Wise Wolf, once again teach us, one and all, and deep in our hearts may we hear your wolf call.

*I*n many ways as we discuss the attributes of Wolf as a totem or power animal, we are talking about different ways that Wolf acts as a guide. This section speaks to Wolf as a *spirit guide* or a *way shower*. This manifestation applies to many different circumstances—not just finding vision or discovering your soul path. Wolf energy may be tapped as an overall guide, and Wolf may, as he has for me, even become one of your main power totems.

I often consult the medicine wheel when communicating with my spirit totems. In the tradition of the medicine wheel, the North shield is thought of as a place of the wisdom of the ancestors, a place of experience. Wolf resides in the realm of the North, and having Wolf in my life means having Wolf guide me as a teacher. Personally, Wolf becomes a powerful teaching medicine when I am working with people both one-on-one and, especially, in groups. When I am teaching or giving a talk, I call upon Wolf to assist me. I ask Wolf Spirit to take me to a place of higher love and wisdom. Wolf retrieves that higher energy—the larger picture—and brings it into my teaching. Even as this book is being created, we look to Wolf for guidance. How would Wolf tell his own story in a way that others in the pack will appreciate and then be compelled to pass on this knowledge?

What is the crux of Wolf's lesson as a guide? Aside from being a totem for becoming better teachers and guides ourselves in general, what does Wolf teach us specifically? As a Wolf Clan elder and one who was deeply connected with Wolf Spirit, Grandmother Twylah revealed this esoteric truth in her teaching. She said that to walk as a Wolf Clan person, you must always, always walk in truth. The truth she spoke of is the inner truth that comes from your *vibral core,* which can be thought of as a dot in the center of your body at the solar plexus. Bisecting this core vertically from above your head to below your feet is your truth line. Horizontally bisecting the core from a length just past your outstretched arms is the Earthpath line. A circle drawn around the core at the four points where these lines end forms your Sacred Space. The North position of the circle is your wisdom, the East houses your integrity, the South gives you stability, and your dignity resides in the West. These four attributes act as anchors that keep your vibral core in spiritual balance. When internal or external disturbances affect your wisdom, integrity, stability, or dignity, the core is unbalanced until you can move through the disruption.

This esoteric Wolf Spirit lesson should not be interpreted as a call for perfect balance at all times. There will always be chaos at times in our lives, as this is part of our shared human experience. There will also be times when we must face the shadow aspects of our personalities, and these shadow lessons are just as vital as walking on a path of light (more on the shadow in the next chapter).

There will always be circumstances that seem beyond our control. The extent to which these situations affect us is, however, completely in our control. For instance, perhaps you are walking on the sidewalk along a busy street. Suddenly there is a violent crash and you find yourself in a moment of time where you can offer help to the injured. In that moment, you can act out of fear, anxiety, or guilt, or you can remain grounded and calm and act in a way that is calm, compassionate, and within your abilities. Perhaps the best you can do is call 911. Perhaps you are trained in CPR or emergency management and take a more active role in assisting the victims. Perhaps, you witnessed who was at fault and are confronted with a choice of speaking the truth or silently walking away. You did not create the accident, but you are still capable of acting from a place of wisdom, integrity, stability, and dignity.

It is by delving into the shadow and confronting the untruths in our lives that we find our way back to the vibral core and our ultimate truth—but only if we intentionally choose a path that leads us there. The longer we avoid our truth, the longer we deal with situations or relationships without standing in wisdom, integrity, stability, and dignity, the more pain and discord we will experience along our journey. As long as we have our Wolf Spirit, we may hold our center, even if our outer life or the world around us is unstable.

Wolf as a guide is also about our capacity to guide and teach others. We can think of our loved ones and even our communities as our equivalent of the wolf pack or our *soul family*. Everyone in our soul families looks to each other for support and guidance, either directly or indirectly through their examples. As we embrace different aspects of Wolf Spirit to help guide us in our relationships and

life circumstances, we teach others by example, whether we like it or not. Gandhi spoke to this truth when he exhorted his followers, "Be the change you want to see in the world." Leadership is not simply an exercise for those in positions of power. Positive change can come from anyone who is walking her path with integrity. Integrity gives validity to whatever we do, and we may call on Wolf's integrity to help us in our roles within our soul families.

Samuel Breidenbach has written on the guide aspect of wolf medicine:

> *Of all the animals available to observe, the wolf stands out as "The Guide." This comes from both ancestor lore and scientific observation. I have personally observed a mated pair with four young cubs and an additional "uncle" attack a grizzly bear (Ursus horribilis) that came too near their den, even though the adult bear outweighed them by more than ten to one, and they succeeded in driving it off. This same group allowed me (an unknown observer) on two occasions to chase them away from their den under a fallen tree, in order to weigh and measure the cubs, with only some threat growling and barking.*
>
> *The difference is "discretion." They know a threat and a non-threat and react accordingly. I have observed this discretion used in many cases to "guide" other members in the pack. Sometimes it is hunting technique. Other times it is how to guard or stand guard. Once, a fox vixen and three cubs were watching a mother wolf (a different grouping) try to teach her cubs to catch mice and voles. It became clear that, instead of seeing the foxes as a potential threat or competitor, the wolf continued the lesson until way after her cubs got it for the benefit of the fox kits as they eventually imitated her in this "game" that had a serious side to it: hunting. This was not the only time I have observed wolves "guiding" others in many ways.*
>
> *Indigenous lore has many stories of wolves teaching other animals and even man how to do various tasks. There are many stories, myths, and legends told about how Wolf taught various tribe members how to do various crucial tasks that ensured the survival of humankind. So the aspect of guide is well established for wolves in many areas.* 🐾

6

Lone Wolf, Shadow Wolf

Lone Wolf, Shadow Wolf

Dark is the night as the cold wind howls through the winter forest covered with glimmering snow, which is the only light that guides your lonely path. Oh Shadow Wolf, you are so far from home, and your pack is no more. You have become the Lone Wolf and must find the place you belong. Onward you go, though you may lose your way—for destiny, or perhaps fate, is calling your name and your DNA. The past has prepared you for what you now face. Your senses are heightened here and now as urgency creeps into your every step. Suddenly, you sniff the air, narrow your eyes, and prick up your ears. For there . . . in the distance, you hear the cries of your new pack not too far away. Shadow Wolf, you must meet this new pack with head and tail held high. No shame do you bring to this fateful encounter. They are waiting for the gift you will deliver to their kin that will make the pack strong again. So run, Shadow Wolf, run. Your time as a Lone Wolf is coming to an end.

What image comes to mind when you think of the lone wolf? Perhaps you think of an outcast animal roaming aimlessly. Maybe the wolf is sick. Maybe images come to mind of an angry wolf prone to attack on a whim. Maybe you think of the metaphorical lone wolf—a person (perhaps even yourself) who doesn't fit in and keeps mostly to himself. In reality, the lone wolf in nature is in a transitional state. When pack dynamics change in a way that forces the wolf out of its role, sometimes it is necessary for it to move on. We have talked about community roles and having a clear, purposeful path in life, and the lone wolf is one who has recognized the need for a new path. In this way, the lone wolf teaches us about having the strength and courage to move into new and sometimes scary uncharted territories for the sake of our own soul purpose, as well as for the sake of others in our communities and soul families. The lone wolf has much to show us about our shadow and how we can access it without allowing it to consume us. Sometimes the journey is not a physical one but rather a journey into parts of ourselves with which we do not identify or that we do not want to claim as our own. Confronting and accepting the shadow aspects of our psyches is one of the scariest and most painful undertakings we can attempt, and Wolf Spirit is a willing ally in this process.

There are times when all of us need solitude. We may feel distracted from our paths because of trying events in our lives or the chaos all around us. It becomes necessary to go inside. In these times in my life, I find it helpful to meditate or engage in a vision quest simply to get away from the fray. It is not, however, anyone's natural state to be perpetually alone and isolated. You or someone you know may have fallen into this rut. They may say, "I am happier when I am alone" or "I feel safer by myself." This comes from a place of being wounded. When people have been abused physically or emotionally—when they feel less-than, when they feel ashamed, when they are caught up in addiction, when they are frightened, if they have been criticized, if they feel like a misfit, if they do not feel accepted, if they have a mental illness or otherwise feel separated somewhat from the rest of society—at such times people naturally withdraw. This attempt to feel invisible to the rest of the world continues until they deal with these issues. This aberration in normal human interaction is shame-based and keeps us from living up to our potential.

One can see this frequently in children when they take on the role of the "bad kid." Such behavior sometimes takes the form of the child becoming the scapegoat, the lost child, or the one who simply "cannot learn." However, the same children who, out of shame, take on these roles are often jealous of the more well-adjusted kids and yearn to fit in somewhere. It is a painful duplicity. We see this played out in the news, when the ostracizing becomes unbearable and ends in suicide. Whether these children are gay, suffer from attention deficit disorder or autism spectrum disorder, are victims of some sort of trauma, are very intelligent or learn differently than other kids, or are very sensitive and not able to cope with social strains, they feel too different and simply cannot find their place in the pack.

This was the situation I found myself in as a child. Looking back, I was very intuitive and psychic. I was not interested in the same things as my peers. I was an only child and felt as though there was no place for me to fit in. I was very sensitive and felt perpetually distracted in school. I did not know how to be a part of the pack. The reasons for this are not absolutely clear. I did not have devastating family issues and, indeed, had loving parents, grandparents, and a network of aunts, uncles, and cousins who gave me a sense of belonging within my family. Part of it may have been certain aspects of my upbringing and being an only child. Some of it may have simply been my uniqueness in a small, rural town with nobody else like me around with whom to bond. One of the first times I really felt like I belonged was in the late 1960s and early 1970s when the hippie movement started. I went away to college and suddenly found my clan, my tribe of people who were "different."

There were things in that movement that were not great for me at the time, including drugs and alcohol, but I found kindred spirits. There were people like me who were idealistic and unconventional—people who were not afraid to express things that went directly against the beliefs and values of the majority of people in my community. I finally felt at home and experienced a great feeling of well-being and belonging. These early experiences (both light and shadow experiences) ultimately led me to where I am today. What I had found was an outer reflection to support who I was. For others, it may be a church group, a recovery group, a political movement, a sports club, or some other network of like-minded people. What is important is that we all need a sense of camaraderie—a sense of knowing that we are not the only one.

To find our kindred spirits, it may become necessary to become a lone wolf for a while. Again, this is not the natural state of things. In the wild, we know that lone wolves have a higher mortality rate than wolves in a pack. The lone wolf is more vulnerable to predators, since he lacks the pack's protection, and to starvation, since he does not benefit from the collaborative pack hunting behavior. The wolf may have been driven out of the pack because of intense competition for food in times of scarce prey or because of competition for a breeding mate. Whatever the reason, the wolf must now successfully transition into another pack for survival. We see here the dual nature of the loner mentality.

It is easy to draw similarities between wolves and ourselves: It will be necessary to go it alone at some points in life, but ultimately we must find a new pack or perish. Being without a pack is at once a painful, lonely time and an opportunity to find our true soul family. By going out on our own, we are able to find kindred spirits. Ultimately, the new, better fit benefits not only the loner but the new pack as well. For wolves, the lone wolf is vital for maintaining or increasing the population. Lone wolves find new packs and fill vacant roles. It has even been observed that they sometimes step into the alpha breeding position in the new pack, asserting dominance over long-established pack members. Even though the importance of the wolf's role in the original pack was so diminished that he served little purpose, he is able to find and fill a vital role in the new pack. This shift enhances the overall strength of both packs and the wolf population in general.

Samuel Breidenbach gives insight into the importance of lone wolf behavior as a means for healthy wolves to transition into a more beneficial role for themselves and for both the original and the receiving packs:

> *The lone wolf is both a metaphor of singular importance and a real occurrence in the wild. This important aspect of wolf behavior has been studied carefully by zoologists and indigenous peoples. While lone wolf behavior may seem strange for a pack-loving animal, it may well be a major insurance strategy for a pack.*

It is certainly a mechanism for dispersal from one generation to the next, as well as a clever survival ploy. The alpha wolves in the pack do not need the conflict of closely related wolves fighting for dominance, which also equates to food sharing and breeding rights. In addition, sometimes they drive members out to preserve the pack, but they are highly unlikely to drive out a sick or weak wolf. So the lone wolf is an important strategy, honed over millennia as an important aspect of wolf behavior. It appears to work like this:

If there is too much competition for game, mates, and territory, a pack uses two separate strategies. First, it breaks down easily into smaller units or subpacks. It may just be a pair or several pairs, or even a couple of brothers or sisters setting off in search of new territory or food resources for a short time. Or it could be just a smaller group with cohesion from a litter. The separating is a way to disperse tensions, still maintain a "pack behavior strategy," and ensure better survival for the group. The pack will usually come back together when more food is abundant and more members are a plus. It may also group together with the coming of winter, when more teeth and paws mean more food. This has been well observed by both scientists and Native peoples, and many human societies have copied this strategy successfully over history.

In the second option, sometimes only a single wolf will set off, and rarely will this individual be seen by the pack again. It is as if they are putting their destiny in the hands of fate or leaving it to Mother Nature's luck of the draw. The lone wolf can be of either gender and any age, young or old, but it is almost never a weak individual. Usually the animal is younger and can fend for itself. Exactly why a lone wolf sets off can only be speculated upon, but a lone wolf is usually a wolf of lower status that has either had enough status fighting or is simply looking for better chances elsewhere—but is still healthy.

This implies that a strategy is at work here. Because the pack is a rigid hierarchy and constant fighting for status can give rise to real sur-

vival issues, leaving to try for higher status elsewhere is a real possibility. But my opinion is that it is more likely a survival mechanism built into the genetic code of the wolf pack.

It is a bold strategy, as a lone wolf in a harsh and often hostile environment is far less likely to survive than an animal that has the protection of the pack. After personal observation over three summers in Alaska, I failed to find any commonality other than that it was almost always a younger member of the pack and an animal in good shape that set off on his own. Perhaps more established members were willing to take their chances with the pack, and the youngsters were risk takers, just as with humans. It does not seem that a wolf is "driven out"; more likely, it chooses to leave. That makes sense, as a weaker pack member of lower status would not long survive without the pack.

The Western myth of wolves driving out members that are weak or unfit pack members does not seem to have much, if any, scientific backing. And there is also anecdotal evidence in the form of nonscientific observations and local stories and legends.

Legends from the Inuit, in Alaska and Canada, tell the story of how the lone wolf goes out with the "blessings" of the pack, as if it is an ambassador from the pack. Scientific observation does not show that this is not the case, so it could very well be true.

Perhaps it is like a flower casting seeds into the wind; while many will fail, only a few—or even just one—is required for the survival of the species. Perhaps wolves know this instinctively and so send out a strong youngster that just might make it, either to find another loner of the opposite sex and start a new pack, or to find another pack in the area (likely related to his or her old pack) that will take him or her in as "new blood."

In this way, should anything happen to the old pack, this "seed" wolf will still carry the genes onward through time. So the lone wolf, in human terms, could also be seen in the context of our ancestors as "The Explorer."

Clearly, the purpose of this behavior is transitional in nature, and not meant to be a perpetual state of being. This is why, in humans, becoming comfortable in the lone wolf state is dangerous. Just as the wolf's chances for survival become exponentially smaller while it is on its own, so we languish psychically and spiritually when we neglect or repress our innate longing to find our soul family. Similarly, what if the wolf wasn't able to recognize the need to strike out on its own? Its role in the pack would be greatly diminished, and the more highly ranked wolves may even strike out against it, forcing it into lone wolf status. We can imagine the wolf feeling like a victim and not understanding why he is being cast out of the circle, only to discover on his path that he has more brilliance than he would have ever known about had he stayed within the pack of origin. Perhaps the evolution of the pack depends not only on the solidness and preservation of the community, but also on the occasional lone wolf that finds a new path. She creates another pack, passing on her DNA and learned wisdom. As humans, we may be able to fool ourselves into complacency because we have achieved more success than a wolf in the wild. Why would one make a substantial change if his outer world is comfortable and appears to be working? This is where Wolf can give us a powerful lesson concerning the shadow.

The shadow is that aspect of ourselves that we have no desire to be, but that we all have the potential to be. The shadow at once represents the darkest reaches of who and what we are capable of being and has the potential to effect powerful transformation in our lives. You might think of the shadow as the villain in a movie. The villain is powerful, and because of his lack of morality, he can consider all the options on the table for advancing his agenda, without regard for loss of property or life. The villain appeals to us because he operates from a place of pure emotional passion, and we long for the kind of reckless power he wields. However, ultimately we do not want to be the villain, and we do not want him to prevail, but that doesn't that mean we can't draw on his dark prowess for lessons in overcoming our own obstacles.

Our shadow may well be a link to our animal selves. Carl Jung believed that the shadow is present in all humans from childhood, but that its primitive nature

is overcome and dominated by our egos. In other words, as we put together the idea of ourselves—of who we are—all of the things that do not fit neatly into a person's idea of "me" are relegated to that person's shadow self. Subconsciously, we acknowledge aspects such as rage or greed, but we store them away and hide them from our conscious selves in the dark layers of the shadow. Rather than owning our shadow, we often project it out onto the world—onto someone else or even collectively onto a whole nation or group of people.

Our shadow is formed in childhood by the desire to be safe, loved, and accepted by those around us. Much of what we put into our shadow depends on the personality and well-being of those closest to us as children. Many people refer to this grouping as our Family of Origin. The patterns that we take from the people in our Family of Origin and the shadows that are created are often dysfunctional and create havoc in later life. The shadow must become more apparent to gain our attention, and when it does, it must be owned and accepted by the individual. This is the only way for a higher level of integration and consciousness to occur. Carl Jung said that much of what is in the shadow is pure gold. In fact, we go through a kind of alchemical transformation in our psyches when we do inner work that involves working with the shadow.

Our shadow consists of qualities that we have exiled into darkness, sometimes unnecessarily due to our own immature judgments about them. After all, the shadow is populated over time, starting at childhood, with rejected notions of ourselves. When we are able to reconcile lost aspects of ourselves from the shadow into our waking consciousness, it is as if we have alchemically turned psychic iron into psychic gold.

Then why is it so difficult to embrace the shadow and draw on its raw power for creativity? The answer is that to own our shadow means to face aspects of ourselves that are perceived as shameful or even disgusting. To accept one's shadow means to surrender to its presence in our unconscious without allowing it to consume us. We can see what happens when people are overcome by the shadow when we look at people in times of emotional distress. War, social unrest, domestic turmoil, and economic emergencies are examples of situations that can bring out the dark nature we all keep in the subconscious layers of our psyches. We project our disgust onto these situations and those involved, often without acknowledging our capacity to sink as low.

Think of the emotions you experience when you see images of the Holocaust, genocide in Africa, looting and rioting after an environmental disaster, gang violence, rape, infidelity, and other negatively charged events and actions. We may see these acts as impossibly evil, but we must understand that they are within our reach. It is important to face our shadows—our capacity for abhorrent behaviors—so that we can integrate them into our consciousness and learn from them.

The wolf has been a reflection of our shadow for millennia. While ancient wolf lore has looked upon the wolf largely in a positive light, the wolf has also been demonized, reflecting those dark aspects of humanity that we do not want to claim as our own. In a way, the shadow aspect of our psyches can be thought of as our alter egos, and perhaps nothing personifies this better than werewolf lore. When we transform into the beast, we lose our sense of self. We become destructive and violent and have the propensity to hurt those we love or indeed anyone who crosses our path. This is a perfect metaphor for allowing ourselves to be overcome by our shadow. The monster is the embodiment of the rejected pieces of ourselves that have been compartmentalized and stored away in the dark recesses. However, what incredible power the monster confers! Can this Shadow Wolf show us a way to access the primal force of our repressed psyches in a way that is healthy and productive?

Working with one's shadow can happen in many different ways. In my work, I take people on inner journeys where, through the power of the breath, an altered state is achieved and the unconscious is brought to the surface. Other people might undergo hypnosis or do work with a transpersonal psychologist. Others may participate in Native American or other indigenous rituals such as the sweat lodge or vision quest. Embracing one's power animal or a spirit animal guide can also be effective. Looking to the wolf, we can mirror the example of surrendering and moving on, as in the lone wolf setting out into the wilderness in search of a new life. Surrender, after all, is giving up control of what we can consciously perceive and trusting whatever the unconscious or the unknown has in store. Surrender is dying to our old ways. It is through sequences of symbolic death and rebirth that the ego learns to surrender to the higher self, what some may call the soul. It is through defeat when all else has stopped working that one makes a change. Most people do not feel a sufficient motive to change prior to the real prospect of defeat. We witness this time and time again in the world around us—that it is only when a bottom has been hit and life becomes sufficiently uncomfortable or even painful that one finds the inner strength to let go of an old reality and truly change.

Dreaming Wolf also plays an important role in shadow work. As previously stated, the shadow lies dormant in the layers of our subconscious and seems to inconveniently show itself when we experience emotional turmoil. To work with the shadow, to confront it on our own terms so as to harness its power for creativity and change, we can look to dreams and other windows into the subconscious. Meditation, guided imagery, Shamanic Breathwork, dream analysis, and sweat lodges are all tools for inner journeys during which we can listen to the unconscious and access archetypal wisdom. Animal totems are ancient and powerful allies to this end as well. Think of wolf as your companion in the spirit world or even in the world of your unconscious. Perhaps you send Dreaming Wolf into the universe to retrieve some lost part of your soul that you dismissed into the shadow long ago. It is important to remember that the shadow contains some of our most powerful gifts as well as that which can be destructive in our lives. Integrating each part of the shadow therefore brings us closer to wholeness and prevents that shadow aspect from unexpectedly sabotaging us. Speaking to the importance of integrating the shadow, Jung said, "I'd rather be whole than good."

Shadow Wolf's ultimate lesson is about becoming whole. We look to Wolf for courage to face our fears and transform our lives—to surrender to that which is unknown or to that which we have buried deep within our subconscious. Perhaps the Shadow Wolf in society is the link we need to move into the next octave for humanity. Wolf sets out to explore new territory and faces obstacles that force him to learn new behaviors of survival and creativity. 🐾

7

Nurture

Gentle Wolf

Thank you, Mother Nature, for sharing your loving energies with the Spirit of the Wolf. Kind wolf, you have been a star student of Nature's wise ways and of her knowledge about how to create perfect balance each day. Gentle wolf, you took on the tall order of teaching her youngest children, the humans, by example how to nurture each other and themselves once again. Long, long ago, oh Wolf Mother and Wolf Father and Sister and Brother, you learned the wisdom of kindness, the balance of friendship and kin. You shared your food, your playtime, and your love with those within your pack again and again.

Without your loyalty and care for each member of the pack they would flounder and perish from Earth and cease to exist. Your generous heart beats heavy in your chest as you eat enough to feed the pups that wait back in the nest. May you continue all of your days to nurture, teach, guide, and play with your family, and long may the power of the wolf pack continue to be!

*W*olves' capacity for love and nurturing is conspicuous when we observe their wild behavior. The pack anticipates a new litter of pups and celebrates enthusiastically with howls and playfulness when they are born. When the pups are old enough to emerge from their den, the pack welcomes them into the family and collectively raises the youngsters as a community. The subordinate wolves take an active role in protecting and teaching younger wolves. Mature wolves can be observed in play behavior that mimics hunting, allowing precocious pups to bite and gnaw at them. The older wolves show tremendous patience and tolerance. Beta wolves have even been observed wet-nursing for the breeding mothers. Above all, the nurturing instinct preserves pack cohesiveness, as the wolf shows a capacity for a larger understanding of what it means to nurture the *idea* of living in a pack. We have seen that when adult wolves are injured, lower-ranking wolves will step into their role, peacefully relinquishing that role when the more dominant animal returns to good health. And we even see the willingness of a wolf to set out on its own when it no longer serves the overall well-being of the pack to remain a part of it.

Regardless of size, strength, color, relationship, or hierarchy, each pack member is nurtured into its eventual role in the community. Once again, our ancestors looked to this behavior for inspiration, and this can be seen in the way indigenous peoples reared their young. In many Native American traditions, the specific abilities of children were noticed and cultivated. The adults paid attention to what the child naturally gravitated toward and developed that child's strengths accordingly. In fact, a child's name was often not given until later in life, since names were highly symbolic. Perhaps if a child was a proficient hunter, he would receive the name He Who Tracks the Deer. Similarly, Cloud Watcher may have been a visionary and a dreamer, destined to become a shaman. Nurturing each child's specific qualities helped that child, right from the beginning, move more fully into who he or she really was instead of attempting to force all into a particular model. Again, doing this nurtures the overall well-being of the pack, tribe, or community so that it can continue to flourish and grow. If a variety of talents are nurtured, the pack acquires all of the components it will need for survival. In this way, individualism is honored, and the pack is better equipped to handle a variety of situations. Each role takes on the spiritual quality of being a sacred part of keeping the community intact.

Looking at all we have learned from Wolf—all the gifts that have been given to humanity—what has Wolf done if not nurtured us through our social and spiritual evolution from our fledgling existence on this planet to the present day? Wolf has inspired us with awe, sparked our imaginations, showed us the rightness of trusting our intuitions, and allowed us to project our darkest fears and short-comings upon it—all of the things selfless and loving parents would do for their children. Perhaps the best way to illustrate the loving, nurturing aspects of wolf medicine is to tell the personal story of how Wolf came into my life as a spirit guide and how I became connected to the Wolf Clan.

Years ago, as I began exploring the spiritual world in more depth, I began having recurring inner visions of the wolf. At the time I had no idea why. I had always loved images and stories of wolves. I felt very drawn to wolves and was never afraid of them. As my interest in Native American studies peaked in the mid-1980s, I began doing work with different teachers around spirit allies, animal totems, and animal guides, and began calling on different guides and helpers. One of the very first and certainly the most powerful animal guide I met was the Wolf. This happened during a guided journey with a Native teacher during which I was encouraged to seek out an animal spirit ally. Wolf revealed itself to me as my main guide, and let me understand that it would lead me to wherever I wanted to go.

Shortly after this revelation, during another guided inner journey, I was in-structed to look for a "spirit grandmother." The person guiding me to do this did so because I had shared with her the close bond I had shared with my maternal grandmother and the devastating loss I felt when she passed away when I was very young. Even though I felt as though we stayed connected after her passing through frequent dreams and visions of her, there was a way in which I so missed my physical grandma. So my teacher suggested that I do a journey with my new-found animal guide, the Wolf, to find my grandma—whether it was my grandma who had gone to the other side or simply a grandmotherly energy—someone

to be there for me, nurture me, and understand me as my grandma had before she passed. I was going through many changes in my life at that time, and I really needed that supportive energy to help me through. I was taking this journey every day for twenty or thirty minutes, and one day I found myself in an underground cave, a kiva. In the extremely lucid but altered experience into which I had dropped, I could feel the cold of the stone cave floor as I sat. I realized suddenly that I had slumped over and was lying with my head in someone's lap. It was such a comforting feeling, and I felt truly nurtured as I felt this person stroking my hair. Even though I was in my thirties at the time, the peace and comfort I felt was clearly that of being in the care of an elder and someone who loved me dearly. At that moment, I heard a voice say to me, "You are a gentle wolf . . . gentle Star Wolf." It felt so right, and somehow I knew she was calling me by a name that was mine! It was a name I had never heard or never considered before then. I looked up at her and then into her eyes and saw that she was a very gentle but strong elder. She did not look familiar, but I knew that we were connected in some way and that she was my spiritual grandmother.

She reminded me of my own grandmother, not in the way she looked but because I sensed the nurturing, supportive energy of my grandmother. There was gentleness but also a kind of wildness to her. It was much to process, and I snapped out of the meditation very quickly. I tried to drop back down into my altered state but was unable to. After the experience, I did some artwork to integrate the vision, and I drew a wolf with a star over its head in the sky with the writing "Gentle Star Wolf."

From that time on and for several years, I tried to figure out if this being I had connected with was real—in this physical world—or if I had encountered her in the spirit world. Eventually, through a series of synchronicities, I ended up putting the pieces together and actually found this spirit grandmother, who turned out to be a real person. This was my first experience with Twylah Nitsch, Seneca Wolf Clan Grandmother. She lived on the Cattaraugus Indian Reservation outside of Buffalo, New York. The first time I met Gram in this physical dimension, I visited at her old family home. She asked me, "What took you so long to get here?" I just laughed and replied, "Well, you didn't tell me what your name was or how to find you!" This would mark the real beginning of our relationship.

We had many encounters over the years, including the several times she visited me in California for the Wolf Song, which brought Peace Elders (Native teachers) together for ceremonies and rituals evoking healing and peace for the world. I also visited her several more times, and we always kept in contact, whether by phone (although Gram despised talking on the phone) or by mail (yes, before the era of electronic communication). Over the years, I soaked in her wisdom and was truly spiritually nurtured by her Wolf Clan teachings. Sadly, in the last few years of her life, I didn't get to spend much time with her, as she had moved to Florida to stay with her family. Gram was approaching her nineties. The last time I visited her, she pulled me very close, looked at me directly in the eyes, and asked, "Star Wolf, are you teaching? Are you sharing the Wolf Clan teachings I have passed to you?" I promised her that I was. Indeed, my work is a weaving together of all of the disciplines I have learned over the years, with her message of walking a path of truth and integrity at the center. Grandmother Twylah passed in August 2007, but at her request, I end all of my ceremonies with a wolf howl to her on the other side.

The nurturing quality of Gram's teachings goes well beyond my personal experiences with her. Her healing message for the world was universal and not restricted to those who followed a specific spiritual path. She wanted the Wolf Clan teachings to live on for what she was convinced are to be very hard times ahead. She loved and was concerned for the Earth, and spoke of the importance of the environment and our relationship with all living things. She spoke of the rock people; the standing people (trees); the four-legged creature teachers; the elemental spirits of water, earth, fire, and air; the winged ones; and everything that swam, crawled, climbed, screeched, howled, and growled. She spoke of the spirit beings of the invisible realms and then us, the two-leggeds. She prophesied that we are now moving out of the fourth era of isolation and separation and into the fifth era of illumination and unity.

Grandma Twylah said that we were about to witness the beginning of the beginning or the beginning of the end. This stuck with me in my head and in my

heart. I choose to believe that humanity is shifting into a new era of love and healing. If this is to come about, we are going to need to live with the qualities of the
Wolf Spirit totem. We will need to embrace leadership and community consciousness. We will need to nurture our resources. Whether or not one feels particularly
drawn to Wolf specifically is not important, but Wolf Spirit embodies the kind of
conscious living needed to bring about change. We must form a new Wolf Clan,
global community, or whatever one may choose to call it. Perhaps it is simply the
One World or One Tribe concept: knowing who we are and our place on the
planet, living in a grounded way, and taking steps to protect and nurture the beautiful gift that is our planet. We can allow the Great Mystery to continue to unfold
and feel the love that Creator has for us all. Everyone and everything is sacred. 🐾

8

Wolf Tales

PEOPLE WHO RUN WITH WOLVES

Anubis

THE ORIGINAL WOLF SPIRIT TOTEM?

Could it be that Anubis, the great jackal-headed deity of ancient Egypt, was an early canid shamanic guide to budding humanity, assisting them in their spiritual and human evolution? In my revelatory work both with Nicki Scully for *Shamanic Mysteries of Egypt* and *The Anubis Oracle* and with Ruby Falconer for *Shamanic Egyptian Astrology*, Anubis repeatedly told me that he was the "first" or "original" on Earth. I have never fully understood the full meaning of what Anubis was trying to tell me; however, I could sense that his words were packed full of esoteric and multilayered meanings and mystery school teachings. Perhaps Anubis really was the first canine shaman on Earth who passed on the original wise spirit teachings to those around him, later inspiring the first Wolf Clans that later spread to many nations and tribes around the world.

The Africa Dogan tribe often referred to the sacredness of the Dog Star, also known as Sirius. The Dog Star has also been called Canis Lupus, and I have heard more than one Native American teacher and friend refer to the Wolf Star, saying that there are certain people who are connected to wolf knowledge and star consciousness who are wisdom carriers of that sacred tradition for the Earth.

Though many people think of the Wolf Clan as mainly belonging to or having its origins with the Native Americans, the Wolf Clan is universal and has been found in many cultures and societies throughout history and perhaps even prehistory. Long before writing was developed, pictographs were drawn on cave walls showing shamans or medicine men and women, draped in wolf skins and heads, dancing or performing sacred rites. When I was in Scotland I met an older gentleman in a country pub who spoke about the Clan of the Wolf. I also spoke to a museum curator about the ancient Celtic Wolf Clan. In the Mayan Calendar tradition, one of the Day Lords is deeply connected to the Spirit of the Wolf. I have not made an extensive study of the many ancient and even modern wolf clans or societies, but I suspect they all have many of the same qualities and shared values.

The image of the wolf, with its long snout, sensitive ears, keen sight, and sharp teeth, can conjure a variety of feelings in the onlooker.

I have always seen the wolf as noble, wise, and beautiful, but I know others who view the wolf with trepidation and as a creature to be feared. We can witness both the admiration and the distaste that the public often displays in both the destruction and the protection of wolves. I have been signing petitions for more than two decades to not only protect wolves but to educate the public and raise awareness of their true nature.

In my Egyptian Mystery School work, I felt in some ways overcome by the spirit of Anubis as he worked through me as a constant guide. Whenever I closed my eyes and called upon him for support and guidance, I downloaded much of the information that was translated into book form with my coauthors and into images with well-known artist Kris Waldherr. In fact, the first image that Kris ever sent to us in order to determine if she would be able to do justice

Anubis

to the images that were showing up in my mind's eye was the beautiful image of Anubis. She nailed it right from the beginning!

During the course of writing this book, in one of the downloading conversations with my son and coauthor Casey Piscitelli, I suddenly felt Anubis speaking to me again, and this time he reminded me in a passionate way that the Spirit of the Wolf has been a longtime and constant guide to humanity. He reminded me that his origins are connected to Sirius, the Dog/Wolf Star system, and that we humans are "star seeds"—as Carl Sagan once said about humanity, we are all made up of "star stuff." Our true home is the cosmos.

Casey had the vision of a very noble and stoic Anubis standing tall while speaking eloquently, with two wise-looking wolves listening intently to his every word. I then had the thought that this was archetypal Anubis who is known in

Egypt as Opener of the Way, instructing our elder four-legged brothers and sisters about how to help humanity to form communities and further our evolution throughout the ages.

This image brought tears to my eyes when I realized that the original Wolf Spirit came from my beloved guide and friend Anubis who, like the wolf, has frequently been misunderstood and seen simply as a fearsome funerary deity or lord of the underworld journey. To me he is so much more: a forerunner of the energy I equate to the Christ energy that is connected to humanity's evolution on all levels. He is the one who teaches us how to shape-shift into higher levels of consciousness and move beyond our limiting lifestyles, addictions, and thought forms. In other words, he constantly guides us compassionately through sequences of symbolic death and rebirth into higher consciousness. He is, for me, quite simply the embodiment of higher love and wisdom—unconditional love—while I am learning how to let go and grow over and over again on the spiral path of human spiritual evolution. His Wolf Spirit teaches me on many levels to remember who I am and who I am capable of becoming.

Anubis helps us to look at ourselves, to see both our shadow and our light, and to become walkers between the worlds of human and spirit. Hopefully, we will learn the lessons we need in order to give birth to a new, divine humanity that was written in the stars long before we were born. Perhaps it is time for the return of the Spirit Wolf Clan as humanity reaches higher for yet another octave on the wheel that is turning and evolving us now. 🐾

Eva Svingen

SEDONA, ARIZONA

After working as a photographer for many years, I created an opportunity for myself to work at a wildlife park in the mountains of Norway, my home country. This wildlife park is in a beautiful location and houses many of the original species of animals (including wolves) belonging to the area in big natural habitats. Since I was a little girl, I have been very fascinated with wolves. I felt like one of them and studied everything I could find through books, movies, documentaries, and while visiting parks and talking with people who lived and worked with wolves. I wanted the chance to be around, or preferably among, the animals that are so fascinating to me. I had visited many wildlife parks and found this one more interesting than others because of the large areas in which the wolves could roam. It was the closest I had seen to wild conditions.

The wolf pack had more than forty acres on which to live. I have never liked seeing wild animals in captivity, and going to a zoo just tears my heart out. The animals at this place were in captivity, but with the large areas and the context of both education and reintroduction into the wild, I felt far less sad than at other places I had visited. After spending a week there with a friend, I proposed to take pictures during a period of a year for them to use in their publicity and for me to use as a freelancer. This is how my journey with the wolves started.

I spent much time studying the wolf pack and waiting for the right shot—the right light or the opportunity to see them at all. It could often take several days. After a period during which I constantly hung around their territory, the wolves seemed to get more used to me and to accept my presence somewhat. I was able to observe how the pack functioned and their hierarchy—the alpha male in front leading and making decisions and the alpha female by his side. There were ten wolves in the pack, and they all knew their place. The alpha male was nine years old when I arrived there and definitely not the physically strongest wolf in the pack, but he was psychologically the strongest and the best leader. His position was not challenged.

I was fascinated with the precise language they used, communicating by positioning their ears and tails. They spoke through submissive behaviors, licking, and other body language, and of course their famous howling, which has triggered feelings of magic and mythology in humans down through the centuries. The pack howls to gather and locate each other, to mark territory, and sometimes just for fun, because they can! The light of the full moon is excellent for hunting, so they take advantage of that. As with those of us who can feel the effects of the full moon, they would also become more energized.

To see how the pack would deal with and behave around new additions of pups was just amazing. I was able to witness this when the alpha female gave birth to four beautiful pups one early-spring morning. She was hiding them in the security of a den, and the whole pack danced around the new pups, brought food, and made sure the mother had what she needed. Later, when the pups were old enough to enter the world outside the den, pack members would play with and care for them in the most patient, loving, and tender way I have ever seen. What a community! I was able to observe this highly functional community for almost two years, wishing I were one of them.

Sadly, there was only room for two more wolves in the pack, as no wildlife park needed any new blood, and there were no reintroduction programs going on. It was decided to take two of the pups out for socialization and education. I was sad about the thought of separating the pups from their mother but excited to be a part of this experience. I volunteered as a surrogate mother right away. Along with one other person, I was now a full-time wolf mother with two beautiful wolf babies, one male and one female: Ask and Embla. We made a little den outside where I could live with my new babies, eight days old and still deaf, blind, and toothless. They would squeak and whine and needed closeness and care 24/7. I went so strongly into the mother role that, after a short while, I actually started to produce milk myself!

After twelve or fourteen days, they opened their eyes, and after nineteen days, they started to focus. They began to hear when they were eighteen days old, and they reacted to every sound around them. Their teeth started to come out at the same time, and suddenly, at only three weeks old, they transformed into small wolves, tearing me up with their claws and teeth, which were as sharp as needles. Their hunting instincts started surfacing, and I will never forget their first squeaky howl on a mountaintop at three weeks old. By the time they were big enough to sink their teeth into raw meat, I did my best to train them as their mother would, holding the piece in my mouth, letting them fight for it, keeping their instincts intact. We slept together, ate together, played together, fought together, howled together, laughed and cried together. It was an amazing experience, and I truly felt like their mother.

I was amazed by their intelligence and their need and ability to carefully observe everything going on around them. They handle things very differently than dogs. Wolves take only calculated risks. Already at three weeks old, they had discovered how things worked around them. They were a beautiful mixture of survival instincts, rational thought, and intuition. When they reached sexual maturity, they started testing me more and more. The instinctual need to know their range and who the alpha was became evident, calling for stricter boundaries and harsher treatment. I had to take the role of the alpha; otherwise, there would be no way to live with the wolves.

I learned so much from these beautiful beings, from both observing the pack and raising the pups. They are a species that lives closest to the way we live, just in a far more functional way. Their teachings are therefore so relevant to us. Their functional packs and hierarchal communities are based on their unique gifts and abilities. The omega wolf has just as important a role as the alpha or anyone in between. The alpha must be the leader. The omega must learn the lessons of the lone wolf and enter or create a new pack. Wolves understand that they are pack animals and that they cannot make it long on their own. The sense of belonging is essential for these animals, as I believe it is for us too. Wolves teach us the importance of community, how to share territory with others in a very meaningful and functional way, and the importance of discovering and sharing our gifts as a part of a society. They express respect, loyalty, boundaries, love, and compassion, and they instinctively know when it is time for self-care. They show a balance of courage and caution, of strength and humility, of self-care and sacrifice, and of loving care and boundaries. Everything they do has meaning and purpose. 🐾

Thea Summer Deer

ASHEVILLE, NORTH CAROLINA

Wolves came into my life more than twenty years ago during a time of transition when my husband, Matohikan, and I decided to move from our home in San Francisco to Tucson, Arizona. We would send most of our belongings ahead in a moving van while taking a detour through Santa Fe to visit a breeder of wolf hybrids. Michael Belshaw, the breeder, had called just days before our move with the news that there were several new litters on the ground. We were ecstatic to learn that we could have our pick! The drive to Santa Fe was haunted with Raven medicine. After several of the birds circled above our car, eventually only one remained, and I felt as though it had a message for me. I cleared my mind and received a message from Raven that a female wolf pup was waiting for me in Santa Fe. The significance of Raven bringing me this message was lost on me at the time, because I was not yet aware of the special relationship ravens share with wolves in the wild. In my memoir, entitled simply *Raven*, I talk more about this relationship:

> *I turned to Matohikan, told him what I had just experienced, and he simply nodded without taking his eyes from the road. When I turned my gaze back toward the raven, it was gone.*
>
> *This all happened long before I learned about the symbiotic relationship between wolves and ravens. Wolves rely on ravens to lead them to the elk, or deer, or caribou. Flying high above the terrain, ravens have the advantage of seeing potential prey down below. In exchange for being a scout for the wolf, raven gets to share in the feast. Their relationship is an intimate one, and they can be found "playing" with each other when not involved in the work of hunting. Wolf researcher L.D. Mech observed that ravens would dive at a wolf's head or tail and the wolf would then duck and leap at them. When the wolf retaliated by stalking the raven, the bird allowed it within a foot before flying away. Shortly it would return, land-*

ing a few feet away from the wolf, and repeat the prank. Both species are extremely social and possess the psychological mechanisms necessary for forming social attachments. Wolves and ravens each seem to be rewarded by the presence of the other and are fully aware of the other's capabilities.

When we arrived at the breeder's ranch, he and his old wolf dog, Chamaco, greeted us. We were led to the pens that housed the pups with their hay-bale dens inside. I noticed another raven that sat as if a sentinel on top of another pen just a little way from us. The raven flew away, scaring all the pups into their dens except for one. The little female was at once scared and intrigued by us. She had the beautiful long-haired traits of her mother, who was part long-haired Buffalo Wolf. She came to the fence and sniffed my face, and we both knew she was coming home with me that day. Her name would be Shash—Navajo for "Bear."

Shash's mother was none too happy with her departure and gave me a bite on the butt as I left the pen with the pup. I heard her loud and clear and understood the responsibility of what I was taking on. Matohikan had also found a companion, although we had come for only one pup. Michael explained to us that it was better to take pups in pairs so they could each have a canine partner. In part, this also helps to ease the pressure on their humans because even in our absence the animals would always have a companion present, which is obviously very important for pack animals. So, along with Shash and the pure white male Arctic tundra wolf now named Chinook ("warm wind from the north"), we set out again for Tucson. That night as we drove through the desert en route to our new home, the pups, having been moved by the sound of a Native American flute on the car stereo, began to howl. Matohikan and I were moved beyond words.

Knowing a wolf or wolf hybrid is not like knowing a dog. Wolves are very gregarious. They bond intensely; as pack animals, they need to be with you all the time; and they are such a responsibility to own. This is why many wolf hybrids end up in wolf sanctuaries. As an owner, you must "show up" for your wolf and truly be its devoted companion. Many wolf owners soon realize that the experience is simply too much to handle.

What I learned from the wolves over the years from observing their behavior was profound. For me, it was like studying human nature because they are so close to us in the way they arrange their family system. Because of my close bond with these wolves, the whole time I had them they mirrored me in a way that always seemed to offer a lesson. That's kind of how it is when you hang out with wolves—things seem to operate on a different level. For example, I bred my wolf hybrids over several generations and thoroughly screened potential buyers, explaining their nature and making sure that the people had the right intentions for owning a hybrid. I had only one wolf come back to the sanctuary, and when I attempted to reintroduce her to the pack, my alpha wolf, her mother, attacked and injured her. At that time, setting and enforcing boundaries in my life was a big issue for me, and the situation was a mirror for the things going on within my own psyche.

Synchronicities surrounding the wolves resulted in some of my most profound moments. During a very difficult separation and divorce I was left with the heavy responsibility of caring for the wolves while dealing with the sadness and loss of my marriage. I opened myself to the universe and prayed for the help I knew I needed. I picked up the local paper and saw a classified ad for a woman who was doing shamanic healing work. Somehow, I immediately knew that she was someone I was supposed to work with. The woman's name is Beverly Laughing Eagle Noble Wolf, and she is a medicine woman with whom I have now worked for more than twenty years. I called her on that day, and before I told her anything about myself or my situation, she said, "Well, I have been expecting your call, because I had a dream about a white wolf last night. Does that have any significance for you?" Taken aback, I responded, "Yes, I have one in my back yard!" The wolf had led me to Beverly, and she eventually became my "mother of choice," just as Michael Belshaw (from whom I purchased my first pair of wolves) had grown to become my "father of choice." The wolf had led me to my pack, my soul family, and to the deep healing that happened for me during that time.

The loving and nurturing qualities of my wolves will stay with me always. Whenever my breeding pair would produce a litter, I was always struck by how the alpha male would always let the mother and pups eat first. He would very carefully hold loving space to make sure the mother and pups were able to eat before he would feed. My wolves and pups were happy and well adjusted. Unless you have heard it for yourself, the sound of wolves and wolf pups singing to the moon is indescribable. Our sanctuary was at the edge of the desert—just miles and miles of open desert—and to hear seven or eight wolf pups learning to howl with their parents into the night sky is simply exquisite.

My experience with owning and breeding wolf hybrids lasted roughly twenty years and recently ended after the last of my wolves passed away from natural causes. The responsibility of owning or breeding wolf hybrids cannot be overstated. There are many irresponsible breeders out there who pay little attention to the temperament of the parents, often producing hybrids that have a tendency toward neurotic behavior. These are the animals that end up in wolf shelters around the world. Personally, owning these incredible animals offered me a chance to build intense, meaningful, and spiritual relationships with them that one simply cannot get by owning dogs. Sometimes people ask about breeding wolves with dogs, and ask my opinion on the ethics of humans owning these animals. I would say that, from this point in my life looking back on my journey with the wolves, I would prefer that they be allowed to live their natural lives in the wild and that we would do better to protect the wild places. I think they allowed themselves to come into our circle in the way that they have, through hybrid breeding, so that we could have a deeper appreciation for who they really are, just as we are learning who we really are. They are powerful mirrors. If we were truly honoring of ourselves, we would leave the wild to the wilderness and protect the wild places within and without. The animals suffer too much at the hands of humans, no matter how much we love them. We would do better to take care of our own with the resources we spend on domesticated animals. And of course this opens the door to a much larger discussion. 🐾

Samuel

TUCSON, ARIZONA

The Furball's eyes were not quite ready to open yet. But when I put my finger near her, she chomped down and started to suck while growling vigorously. I immediately heard the name Tasha in my mind, and so that became her name. Her parents had been shot just outside Denali National Park in Alaska, and she was one of five wolf cubs needing desperate attention.

As a zoologist studying wolf behavior in Alaska and working toward my masters degree in evolutionary zoology, I was one of the people called by a state agency. Tasha had been turned over to the agency by a tender-hearted indigenous family who had found the pups. So I was a new daddy. Technically, this was against the rules and regulations, but no one wanted these precious little creatures to perish from neglect. So the way was smoothed for me to "temporarily foster" an Alaska gray wolf pup.

That fostering lasted for seven and a half years and was one of the most rewarding and challenging events in my life. Wolves are clearly a highly superior form of life. I had studied them for a few years—first as a volunteer, then as a scientist, and finally as a caretaker. This amounted to a firsthand observation by a trained researcher—a situation that has rarely been presented to a scientist or a modern human. While it is not absolutely rare for a scientist to observe wolves in the wild, it is uncommon, and it is unusual, even rare, for a trained person to observe a single pack or individual for years. As a trained wolf zoologist, I have both seen them in the wild for extended periods (in Denali National Park and Preserve) and lived 24/7 for more than seven years with an orphan born to wild parents. I picked up communication techniques that I later found to be effective with wild wolves, learned the adaptive behavior a "socialized" wolf is capable of (such as learning games and even making up and teaching humans wolf games), came to understand their sense of humor and jokes, and observed their extremely high intelligence.

I already knew that the first few weeks and, to a slightly lesser extent, the next few months were critical to the socialization of wolves. I had learned this through meticulous observations in the field and correspondence with other researchers throughout North America. So I arranged to be with Tasha 24/7 for this time. I believe that this very close social interaction was the key to her developing into a fine companion, albeit one with some quirks.

Bonding must occur, and then a pack hierarchy must be established; otherwise, future problems will be nearly impossible to deal with. This is a wild animal with strong genetics for survival. Would she be able to adapt to a basically urban or suburban lifestyle as her ancestor, the dog, did so well? Would there be problems in her adapting to mankind's world?

As it turned out, the answer was a conditional yes, but her strength of character came though when needed. A wolf is not just a "super dog," but a superior creature of incredible intelligence, strength, adaptability, and even a sense of humor. In the wild, scientists have observed wolves playing tricks on each other and other animals, and I can confirm that they do indeed have a mischievous nature reflecting their very high intelligence and understanding of all that is going on around them.

Here are some incidents from Tasha's life that illustrate her complex nature. Her "killer instincts" were difficult to deal with. She was a hunter and always alert to food around her, at least as she perceived it. As an example, a pet parrot that walked up to her was simply another "chicken" that should go down her gullet. A parakeet flying in the air was just a meal on wings to her. And a cat walking through her yard was one more snack, whether it sat still or tried to run. All simply became lunch, to our horror.

And yet she did understand the concept of "living nonfood," as she would tolerate several of our pet cats so long as she could put her paws onto them or roll on them occasionally, which I believe was simply to establish dominance and to mark what was "hers." She would even defend them from someone else whom she didn't know and accept. She absolutely understood what was hers and what belonged to others, in terms of what I would call ownership.

Another extremely interesting behavior was "play." Zoologists tell us that play, as learning, is an almost universal trait found in the so-called higher animals. Tasha understood about play far better than any dog or cat I have ever observed. Not only could I show her a game, such as fetch, tug of war, or hide and seek, and have her learn the rules incredibly quickly, but she actually made up her own games and taught them to her dumb mammal companion (me), or at least tried to.

The rules of her games often had a wolf intelligence factor that left me somewhat confused as to what they were. But she sure knew how to teach them. If I made a mistake or "cheated," she would quickly punish me. I found out the hard and painful way the consequences of cheating or rule-breaking during one game, after an infraction that wasn't even deliberate. She cocked her head to the side, as if assessing the severity of the penalty; then, before I could move, she bit my elbow, but without drawing blood. Still, I couldn't use that arm for a good fifteen minutes. I had seen similar behavior in the wild when an adult punished a cub, but being on the receiving end was another thing altogether. I knew that the wolf had the strongest bite recorded for a land animal, but it has to be experienced to be believed.

The strength of her bite was astounding. Grizzly bears, mountain lions, and other similar carnivores also use their paws, but wolves rely almost exclusively on the power of their jaws. She had done the same to my leg as well once before in play, and now I know how their hunting strategy works on even a moose, which severely outweighs them. Observing has to sometimes take a back seat to experiencing, and on that day Tasha taught me in spades.

Apparently there are a lot of genetics in a wolf's behaviors, even though they are great at learning and adapting to circumstances. One time I took her to a river, and within minutes she had figured out how to jump beyond a fish and herd it up onto shallow water where she could grab it for lunch. I certainly never taught her that. She just figured it out, and I believe it was from a deep genetic memory or knowing.

Perhaps one of the most amazing skills she possessed was the ability to determine in seconds if a stranger was "good" or "bad." Only three times did she really object to an individual whom she met. And I mean really object, growling deep and lunging to bite if not held back. In all of these three cases, the person later did or tried to do me some damage. One burglarized my place. Another tried to attack a female companion. And the last guy tried to con me. How could she know what might happen in the future? I can't answer that, but facts are facts.

These are just a few of my direct observations of her seven and a half years with me. When she was seven years old she developed cancer, and I believe it was because I fed her too much commercial dog food and not enough raw meat, but I will never know. After treatment, and when we thought she had recovered, she was at the veterinarian with me and watching me intently, for what I don't know. But all of a sudden, and for the first time in her life, she reached over and bit the vet and drew blood.

This was the end of her sojourn on this plane, as the medical professional insisted that she be put down and tested for rabies (off with her head, said the white queen); we were informed that a legal impounding would result if we didn't cooperate. Clearly the clever and supersmart wolf knew what her actions would entail, and who am I do dispute the rules of her game?

I believe she knew she was going to die, as the test showed no rabies but a return of the aggressive cancer. Did she know? How could she have? But that question had remained with me deeply after that day, until not long afterward she showed up one night in my dreams. In this dream, she was in another form. She and her mate were cloud-running shape-shifters, and she was called Shatasha. She told me she was very happy as a wind-walking Wandesha. (According to shamanic lore, the Wandesha, also called wind-walkers or sky-runners, are wolves and sometimes other carnivores who "deserve," by virtue of their superior lives in the Middle World or physical realms, to go to the equivalent of wolf heaven.) In that memorable dream, or dream vision, she agreed to be my guide and was my first power animal.

She is still with me today, though there is no science in that statement. I know what I know, and I would have it no other way. Wolves are, in my opinion, teachers and "herders" of mankind. At least for those of us who allow it. The story is not over, but this is the basic structure of my experience with an exceptional wolf named Tasha. Be careful what you wish for as a child, for you may get it beyond your wildest dreams—or not! 🐾

Afterword

In the Lakota tradition, the phrase *Aho Mitakuye Oyasin* refers to the sacred connection between all things; literally, it means "all my relations" or "all are related." A traditional Lakota poem has the phrase as its title.

Aho Mitakuye Oyasin
All my relations. I honor you in this circle of life with me today. I am grateful for this opportunity to acknowledge you in this prayer . . .
To the Creator, for the ultimate gift of life, I thank you.
To the mineral nation that has built and maintained my bones and all foundations of life experience, I thank you.
To the plant nation that sustains my organs and body and gives me healing herbs for sickness, I thank you.
To the animal nation that feeds me from your own flesh and offers your loyal companionship in this walk of life, I thank you.
To the human nation that shares my path as a soul upon the sacred wheel of Earthly life, I thank you.
To the Spirit nation that guides me invisibly through the ups and downs of life and for carrying the torch of light through the Ages, I thank you.
To the Four Winds of Change and Growth, I thank you.
You are all my relations, my relatives, without whom I would not live. We are in the circle of life together, co-existing, co-dependent, co-creating our destiny. One not more important than the other. One nation evolving from the other and yet each dependent upon the one above and the one below. All of us a part of the Great Mystery.
Thank you for this life.

I have learned that there are no coincidences—only synchronicities. If you found this book, it means Wolf found you and is inviting you to hear his ancient call, helping you remember dormant yet instinctual truths.

Wolf offers us many lessons, but the most powerful of these is love. Love's power is derived from its limitlessness. Wolf teaches us that expanding our consciousness and accepting all of creation as our true family—animals, plants, rocks, the heavens, the elements, our spirit guides—expands our capacity for love and for creating positive change in the world. Charles Eisenstein, the author of *Sacred Economics* (2011), said, "I think love is the felt experience of connection to another being. An economist says that, essentially, more for you is less for me, but the lover knows that more for you is more for me too. If you love somebody then their happiness is your happiness. Their pain is your pain. Your sense of self expands to include other beings. That's love. Love is the expansion of the self to include the other."

Wolf's wisdom can help us dissolve the barrier we have built over time that obscures the truth about our interconnectedness with nature. And when this barrier is removed, we can begin to perceive all of nature as part of our soul family and not as the "other." We can have gratitude and view our Earth and her wonders not simply as resources to be divvied up and squandered but rather as our soul family, offering us their sacred gifts to be shared and appreciated. This change in perception can help us become whole. Cultivating this awareness is the way we can repay the debt we owe to nature for generously tending and preparing the Earth for millennia in anticipation of our arrival. Once, we were a perfect fit. Once, humans occupied our unique niche in nature. It is now our responsibility, using all of our creativity, intellect, love, and awareness, to again find our perfect place in the scheme of Great Mystery. ❧

Index of Art

Wolf Resources

CALIFORNIA WOLF CENTER

The California Wolf Center is a 501(c)(3) nonprofit wildlife education center committed to increasing public awareness and understanding of the importance of all wildlife by focusing on the history, biology, behavior, and ecology of the gray wolf (*Canis lupus*). The center offers engaging educational presentations, participates in conservations programs, and hosts and funds research on both captive and free-ranging wolves.
http://www.californiawolfcenter.org

DEFENDERS OF WILDLIFE

Founded in 1947, Defenders of Wildlife is one of the country's leaders in science-based, results-oriented wildlife conservation. The organization is committed to saving imperiled wildlife and championing the Endangered Species Act, the landmark law that protects plant and animal life.
http://www.defenders.org
http://www.facebook.com/DefendersofWildlife

FULL MOON FARM WOLFDOG SANCTUARY

Full Moon Farm is an organization dedicated to the well-being of the wolfdog. Situated on 17 beautiful mountain acres in Black Mountain, North Carolina, it operates as a federally recognized 501(c)(3) nonprofit organization for abused and refused wolfdogs who find themselves in need of love, shelter, and care through no fault of their own.
http://fullmoonfarm.org/cms/
http://www.facebook.com/#!/pages/Full-Moon-Farm-Wolfdog-Sanctuary/208635945835968?s
k=info

INTERNATIONAL WOLF CENTER

The International Wolf Center advances the survival of wolf populations by teaching about wolves and their relationship to wild lands, and about the human role in their future. The center envisions a world in which populations of wolves thrive, well distributed in many parts of their native range. A global system of designated wild lands supports abundant habitat and prey for wolves and other large carnivores.
http://www.wolf.org

NATIONAL WILDLIFE FEDERATION

The National Wildlife Federation is America's largest conservation organization. It works with more than 4 million members, partners, and supporters in communities across the country to protect and restore wildlife habitat, confront global warming, and connect with nature.
http://www.nwf.org/Wildlife/Wildlife-Library/Mammals/Gray-Wolf.aspx

ROB GUDGER AND WOLF TALES

Rob graduated from North Carolina State University with a degree in wildlife biology. He is a hunting and outdoor enthusiast who encourages everyone to get out and experience nature firsthand. During the school year he takes his show on the road, making presentations to school children, teens, adults, and seniors.

http://www.facebook.com/pages/Trapper-Rob-WolfTales/221091754592464?sk=a
pp_108786665880886

UK WOLF CONSERVATION TRUST
The trust has at its core four main objectives: to enhance public awareness and knowledge of wild wolves and their place in the ecosystem, to provide opportunities for ethological research and other research that may improve the lives of wolves both in captivity and in the wild, to raise money to help fund wolf-related conservation projects around the world, and to provide wolf-related education programs for young people and adults.
http://ukwct.org.uk

VENUS RISING ASSOCIATION FOR TRANSFORMATION AND UNIVERSITY FOR SHAMANIC PSYCHOSPIRITUAL STUDIES
We are a 501(c)(3) nonprofit spiritual organization and university dedicated to transforming personal and planetary consciousness during this great shift of the ages and supporting people in truly stepping into their soul purpose on the planet at this time.
http://www.shamanicbreathwork.org
venus@shamanicbreathwork.org
(828) 631-2305
P.O. Box 486, Sylva, NC 28779

WILDLIFE CONSERVATION NETWORK
The Ethiopian Wolf Conservation Program of the Wildlife Conservation Network alleviates threats to Ethiopian wolves by monitoring their numbers and protecting the areas where they live. The program vaccinates domestic dogs to effectively control the spread of disease; it also has created a comprehensive education campaign for local schoolchildren and employs many local residents, raising the standard of living and fostering a strong conservation ethic among those who most closely co-exist with this rare carnivore.
http://wildlifeconservationnetwork.org/wildlife/ethiopianwolf.html

WOLF CONSERVATION CENTER
Founded in 1999, the Wolf Conservation Center is a 501(c)(3) nonprofit organization that promotes wolf conservation by teaching about wolves, their relationship to the environment, and the human role in protecting their future.
http://www.nywolf.org

WOLF HAVEN INTERNATIONAL
Wolf Haven International is a 501(c)(3) nonprofit organization that has worked for wolf conservation since 1982. The group's mission is to conserve and protect wolves and their habitat. Over the past 29 years, Wolf Haven has rescued and provided lifetime sanctuary to more than 160 animals.
http://www.wolfhaven.org

WOLFQUEST
The Minnesota Zoo and eduweb.com have partnered to develop *WolfQuest*, an innovative project that brings the immersive, compelling drama and action of video games to informal science learning, and to create a model for nationwide distribution. Designed for players age nine to adult, *WolfQuest* teaches wolf behavior and ecology through exciting gameplay and intense social interactions.
http://www.wolfquest.org

Acknowledgments

We would like to thank:

The staff of Sterling Publishing, especially our gifted editor, Kate Zimmermann, both for following her wolf's nose and finding us and for being supportive throughout the process of writing this book.

Our copyeditor, Patricia Fogarty, for her thorough fine-tuning.

Antonia Neshev, for capturing the varied aspects of the Spirit of the Wolf in her stunning artistic renderings.

Samuel Breidenbach, for his visionary wolf insights, which combine science and shamanism.

Eva Svingen, for her uncanny ability to connect to the hearts and minds of wolves.

Thea Summer Deer, for eloquently sharing her mystical and deeply personal adventures with her wolf hybrids.

Our partners, Brad Collins and Jenny Dockrey, for their patience, excitement, and consistent support during the process.

Richard and Dorothy Finley, for their unwavering faith in us.

Aidan Rayne and Cian Sky Piscitelli, and Anthony and Michael Contreras, our special boys who know the magic of wolf medicine.

Our spirit daughter/sister, Laura Wolf, for hearing the call and holding the vision.

Our adopted wolf pups, Ryland, Thomas, Madeline, Bliss, Nizzie, Sophie, Augusten, and Veda.

Mammy Jones, for being the first to teach me the mysteries of communicating with my animal allies.

Grandmother Twylah Nitsch, Seneca Wolf Clan grandmother, for her wolf howls that continue to echo from the other side.

The numerous Wolf Clans of all cultures, spanning across time and geography since antiquity, for passing the wisdom teachings to each new generation.

Friends, students, and soul family (Wolfies) of Venus Rising Association for Transformation.

Derek Chance Thomasson, for providing sacred space and his loyal friendship.

Jessica Cook, soul sister.

Robin Piscitelli, for his free spirit.

All of the individuals and organizations that continue to honor and protect wildlife and wild spaces.

Anubis, the jackal-headed god of ancient Egypt, for his inspiration and for being perhaps the first of the canine spirit guides.

Our four-legged companions, Vision Wolf, Bodhi, Goose, Anubis, Lakshmi, Bob, and Pookie—for their unconditional love and for keeping us wild.

And the eternal Spirit of the Wolf—teacher, guide, elder brother/sister—which has lasted through the ages to renew the best qualities of humanity, as we continue on our evolutionary journey.

About the Authors

LINDA STAR WOLF, the creator of Venus Rising Association for Transformation and the Shamanic Breathwork™ Process, is the founder and president of Venus Rising University for Shamanic Psychospiritual Studies and the Shamanic Minsters Global Network. A spiritual granddaughter of Seneca Wolf Clan grandmother Twylah Nitsch, Star Wolf is the author of *Visionary Shamanism*, *Shamanic Breathwork*, and *30 Shamanic Questions for Humanity* and co-author of *Shamanic Egyptian Astrology*, *Shamanic Mysteries of Egypt*, and *The Anubis Oracle*. She lives at Isis Cove Community and Retreat Center near Asheville, North Carolina. She is also the spiritual director for Transformation House Soul Recovery Program, a facility that provides a safe place and a supportive process for those desiring intensive mind–body–spirit transformation.

http://www.shamanicbreathwork.org
venus@shamanicbreathwork.org
Blog: aquarianshaman.lindastarwolf.com
Transformation House website: vratransformationhouse.org
(828) 631-2305
P.O. Box 486
Sylva, NC 28779

CASEY PISCITELLI is a shamanic minister through Venus Rising Association for Transformation as well as a contractor. He resides in western Kentucky and has been a contributor to other publications by his mother, Linda Star Wolf, including *Shamanic Breathwork*, *30 Shamanic Questions for Humanity*, and the forthcoming *Instar Medicine Wheel*.